PRACTICAL DRAMA HANDBOOK

Rosemary Linnell

HODDER AND STOUGHTON
LONDON   SYDNEY   AUCKLAND   TORONTO

British Library Cataloguing in Publication Data

Linnell, Rosemary
  Practical drama handbook.
  1. Theatre. Production — Manuals
  I. Title
  792'.0232

  ISBN 0-340-48708-9

First published 1988

© 1988 Rosemary Linnell

All rights reserved. No part of this publication may be reproduced or transmitted in any form or by any means, electronically or mechanically, including photocopying, recording or any information storage or retrieval system, without either the prior permission in writing from the publisher or a licence permitting restricted copying. In the United Kingdom such licences are issued by the Copyright Licensing Agency; 33–34 Alfred Place, London WC1E 7DP. *However, permission is granted for photocopying of this book in schools.*

Designed by Wendi Watson

Typeset in Great Britain by Photo Graphics, Honiton, Devon.
Printed in Great Britain for Hodder and Stoughton Educational, a division of Hodder and Stoughton Limited, Mill Road, Dunton Green, Sevenoaks, Kent
by St Edmundsbury Press, Bury St Edmunds,
Suffolk

Acknowledgements

The author is especially indebted to the work of David Davis, Gavin Bolton and Bert Parnaby.

The author and publishers would like to thank the following for permission to reproduce extracts from copyright texts: page 16–17, Paul Sills, *Story Theatre*, copyright ©, 1971, by Story Theatre Productions Inc.; page 21, Bertold Brecht, translated by James and Tania Stern and W. H. Auden, *The Caucasian Chalk Circle*, Methuen London; pages 28–29 copyright © 1968 Arthur Miller and Ingeborg M. Miller, Trustee, *The Price*, Penguin Books Ltd and Viking Penguin Inc.; page 38, George Orwell, the estate of the late Sonia Brownell Orwell, *Nineteen Eighty-Four*, Secker & Warburg Ltd; page 39, Harold Pinter, *The Birthday Party*, Methuen London; page 42, Roger McGough, 'The Fight of the Year', reprinted by permission of A. D. Peters and Co. Ltd; page 44, Sue Townsend, *The Secret Diary of Adrian Mole Aged 13¾*, Methuen London; page 49, Barbara Smucker, *Underground to Canada*, reprinted by permission of Irwin Publishing, Canada; page 50, Peter Townsend, *The Smallest Pawns in the Game*, Grafton Books; pages 63–64, Anne Frank, *The Diary of Anne Frank*, reprinted by permission of Vallentine Mitchell & Co. Ltd; page 65, Barry Hines, *A Kestrel for a Knave*, Michael Joseph Ltd; page 81, Jules Feiffer, *Hold Me!*, reprinted by permission of The Lantz Office, New York; page 82, Dylan Thomas, *Under Milk Wood*, Dent, reprinted by permission of David Higham Associates Ltd; page 87, Christopher Fry, *The Boy with a Cart* (1945), Oxford University Press; page 102, Thom Gunn, 'Moly', Faber and Faber Ltd; page 104, Dylan Thomas, 'And Death shall have no Dominion', Dent, reprinted by permission of David Higham Associates Ltd. We would be grateful for help in tracing the author or copyright holder for the material on pages 18–19, from Leslie Paul's 'The Living Hedge', published in *A Scrapbook of London Life*, ed. Esmor Jones, Blackie (1975).

The photographs in this volume are reproduced by kind permission of the following: David Linnell, who took the photographs on page 99, 101 (photograph a), 103, 105 and 106; BBC Hulton Picture Library for the portraits on pages 20, 64 and 85; Sally and Richard Greenhill Photo Library for the photographs on pages 24 (bottom), and 25 (top); Topham Picture Library for the photographs on pages 25 (bottom) and 27 (top); Pacemaker Press, Belfast for the photograph on page 24 (top); Brian Shuel Photo Library for the photograph on page 27 (bottom); Donald Cooper Stage Photography for the photograph on page 45; Popperfoto (Reuter's Photo Library) for the photograph on page 66; Dr Barnardo's Photographic Archive for the photographs on pages 70 and 71, and the etchings of destitute children on page 69; Network Photographers for the photograph on page 72; The Japan National Tourist Organisation for the photograph on page 101 (photograph b); Mr Ken Corsbie for the photograph on page 104; The British Museum Photograph Library for the photograph on page 107; The Mansell Collection for the photograph on page 109 (top). We would be grateful for help in tracing the copyright holders for photographic material on pages 86, 102, 108 and 109 (bottom).

Contents

Introduction	The purpose and layout of the book	6
UNIT 1	TELLING A STORY	8
Lesson 1	The vocabulary of drama	8
2	Constructing a story	10
3	Narrative theatre	11
4	The details of a story	12
5	Selecting the scene	13
Resource sheet 1	Newspaper and magazine headlines	15
2	The Poor Peasant and the Cow I	16
2A	The Poor Peasant and the Cow II	17
3	The Night the World Ended I	18
3A	The Night the World Ended II	19
4	Bertold Brecht	20
5	The Caucasian Chalk Circle	21
6	Time to Go Home I	22
6A	Time to Go Home II	23
7	Photographs: role-play	24
8	Aristotle	26
9	Fight for youth felled by sword	27
10	The Price I	28
10A	The Price II	29
	Student Assessment Form Unit 1	30
UNIT 2	WHAT IS THEATRE?	31
Lesson 1	Concentration	31
2	Fights	32
3	Body language	34
4	Movement, voice and ritual	35
5	Assuming a character	36
Resource sheet 11	Nineteen Eighty-Four	38
12	The Birthday Party	39
13	Romeo and Juliet I	40
13A	Romeo and Juliet II	41
14	Poem: The Fight of the Year	42
15	Ageing figures	43
16	The Secret Diary of Adrian Mole	44
17	The Pilgrim's Progress I	45
17A	The Pilgrim's Progress II	46
18	Mask-making instructions	47
19	AB scene	48
20	Underground to Canada	49
21	The Smallest Pawns in the Game I	50
21A	The Smallest Pawns in the Game II	51
21B	The Smallest Pawns in the Game III	52
	Student Assessment Form Unit 2	53

	UNIT 3	WORKING CREATIVELY AS PART OF A GROUP	54
Lesson	1	Trust 54	
	2	Group identity 56	
	3	Communication and understanding 58	
	4	The group under pressure 60	
	5	The individual within the group 61	

Resource sheet	22	The Diary of Anne Frank I 63
	22A	The Diary of Anne Frank II 64
	23	Kes 65
	24	Kidnap girl freed in dawn raid 66
	25	'Foreign immigration form' 67
	26	'English immigration form' 68
	27	Drawings of Dr Barnardo's work 69
	28	Dr Barnardo's children I 70
	28A	Dr Barnardo's children II 71
	29	Youth shelters in concrete boot 72
		Student Assessment Form Unit 3 73

	UNIT 4	BUILDING A CHARACTER 74
Lesson	1	Establishing a base 74
	2	One in a crowd 76
	3	Physical characteristics 77
	4	Character motivation 78
	5	Building a crowd scene 80

Resource sheet	30	Jules Feiffer monologues 81
	31	Under Milk Wood 82
	32	The Fall of Troy I 83
	32A	The Fall of Troy II 84
	33	Anton Chekhov 85
	34	Konstantin Stanislavsky 86
	35	The Boy with a Cart 87
	36	Launcelot Gobbo 88
	37	Illustration: Only a child run over 89
	38	Text from A Tale of Two Cities 90
		Student Assessment Form Unit 4 91

	UNIT 5	PERFORMANCE AND A STUDY OF THE ACTOR–AUDIENCE RELATIONSHIP 92
Lesson	1	The Lotos-Eaters 93
	2	Circe 94
	3	The Descent into Hades 95
	4	The Sirens, Scylla and Charybdis 95
	5	The Homecoming 96

Resource sheet	39	Odysseus and the Lotos Isles 99
	40	Poem: The Lotos-Eaters 100
	41	Circe 101
	42	Poem: Moly 102
	43	Hades 103
	44	Poems on death 104
	45	Sirens, Scylla and Charybdis I 105
	45A	Sirens, Scylla and Charybdis II 106
	46	Greek vase illustration 107
	47	The Homecoming I 108
	47A	The Homecoming II 109
		Student Assessment Form Unit 5 110
		Pro Forma Teacher Assessment Form 111

Introduction

It is not possible to construct a syllabus or course that will satisfy the needs of every teacher and every class. There are, however, certain elements that are common to most drama syllabuses. By picking out those fundamental elements and building them into a course that moves from one stage to another in accessible units of work, it is possible to establish something that may serve those teachers who have drama on their timetables.

Most of the material in this coursework pack is aimed at the student who is relatively new to drama and most of it is intended for students in secondary education. Because it is a fundamental drama course, much of the work is neither new nor original. All the ideas have been worked on and tried out by experienced drama teachers, but ample room has been allowed for experiment within the basic course framework. The teacher and drama group can therefore extend themselves in any direction that seems appropriate, whilst still finding a logical progression through their studies. It is important that timetabled drama is seen to progress and that achievement can be, in some way, measured. For this reason the minimum of 'one-off' lessons is offered while a large number of related pieces of material have been included which can be used in a variety of ways.

The drama and theatre arts coursework in this pack is designed in five major units. It may be that the five units will be worked in five half-terms to make up a one year, concentrated course. It is also possible that the work will be spread over five whole terms, to fit the more usual two-year pattern of studies.

The course begins straight away with the related theme work. Teachers who find themselves with an entirely new group who do not normally work together, and who do not know or trust the teacher, may wish to spend some time on trust exercises or 'name games'. This is one of the reasons why the course contains five and not six units. It has been designed to allow time for such preparation work as well as for polishing and refining certain elements whenever necessary.

Each unit contains five sub-sections. Every sub-section allows for one planned lesson, with suggestions for follow-up work. Some sections require more space and facilities than others, but much of the work may be done in a classroom, so long as desks can be moved. It is entirely the choice of the individual teacher as to how much time is given to each section; there is a logical development over the whole course, but the teacher and the group may wish to re-arrange the work into a more suitable pattern according to everyone's aims and requirements. In the coursework there is room for regular self-assessment by students, as well as suggestions for further written work and reading or research. It may well be that these have to be spaced out over more than five, or even ten, lessons but it is important that some reading and writing are included throughout the course even if only in order to prepare for any possible examination. Photocopiable forms for students' written assessment of their work are provided at the end of each unit. The pro-forma assessment at the end of the pack may be useful to the teacher who wishes to keep a record of the individual student's progress through the course, whether or not the pack is used as part of an examination syllabus.

A good deal of equipment is suggested throughout the pack; however, most of the work may be done without any equipment at all. Every student will require a file or folder in which to keep written work and memorabilia. Writing materials are essential for most sections and drawing paper for some of the work, while building blocks and cardboard for models are useful, as well as the usual full-size rostra where those are available in the drama room. Cassette or tape recorders feature largely in the work, especially in the follow-up sections. These are especially useful with students who find writing difficult. The recordings may need to be transcribed for their folders at a later date but tape is a useful way of keeping a record of a piece of work.

As well as lesson-plans and exercises, each of the five units contains resource material, printed separately, so that teachers may reproduce it and have copies available for everyone. Some of this is stimulus material, some of it is technical, practical or pictorial, and as such may be needed for the students' own folders. All resource material required or suggested for each lesson will be found listed with that lesson's preparation notes.

Performance is one of the fundamental elements in the work and is usually seen in the form of immediate communication of ideas and methods to other people in the group (including the teacher). Public performance is implicit in some of the work, but this is a matter for the group to decide.

Practical work is designed to be introduced by the teacher, and the timing and organisation of the group's work is entirely a matter for the teacher to decide. Within any class there may be times when it is desirable for some students to engage all the attention of the teacher whilst others may wish to get on by themselves.

Unit 1 Telling a Story

Unit 1 is concerned with the way drama uses narrative. Students often try to put the whole story into their plays, thereby running the danger of becoming very tedious and of losing the emphasis of what they want to say. This unit therefore includes a variety of narrative styles and concentrates on the techniques involved in structuring a play so that it tells an effective story.

Listening and watching are important skills in drama work. Most of the exercises in this unit involve tasks for the audience as well as for those who are communicating their ideas. Because the audience is seen as a necessary check on the effectiveness of a chosen method of story-telling, it should be possible to elevate the status of those people who are watching, thus creating a mood of creative criticism from the start.

LESSON 1

The Vocabulary of Drama

The first lesson consists of a number of short exercises aimed at building an awareness of the vocabulary of drama and a system of demonstrating the students' understanding of the components of dramatic structure. By focusing on the word 'drama', students may be encouraged to be sensitive towards such concepts as dramatic tension, conflict, heightened forms of expression and the elements that make an ordinary event into a drama. In their discussions they may come across other words which have a dramatic connotation, and these may be recorded for further reference. Such words as 'theatrical', 'scene', 'characters', may well be written up around the drama room as they occur in discussion thereby stimulating the collection of further examples from newspaper headlines, and incidentally establishing a vocabulary for later written work.

Preparation

```
RESOURCE SHEET 1
Paper and pencils
Optional:
Indoor camera
Strong light source
```

Students will need copies of resource sheet 1. They will also need paper and writing materials and ideally someone should have a camera that is capable of taking good indoor pictures. In enabling the students to set up the 'photographs' or tableaux that are included in the exercises, a 'spotlighting' technique might be exciting. A single light source, such as a slide projector, could be used to focus the attention of the audience on the images chosen by the students. It may also be effective to backlight their images so that they appear in silhouette.

The first discussion may need to be firmly directed by the teacher. With a very new group it could be important to hold an introductory discussion of the way drama is perceived by the teacher and the pupils and the necessary rules of conduct in the drama room, before going into the uses of dramatic terms in our everyday language. A more experienced group may wish to begin considering the resource material at once. After the initial introduction the group work may be private and need no teacher intervention at all.

Practical Work

1 What is drama?
Newspaper reporters employ the word 'drama' to catch readers' interest. They may describe an incident as dramatic and we usually accept this as evidence of a certain style

of writing, but if we can analyse what the word means we should be able to create something that will catch other peoples' attention in much the same way as newspaper headlines attract our attention and encourage us to find out more. The class may split up into small groups or the teacher may wish to keep them all together to discuss the way the word 'drama' is used in the newspaper headlines on resource sheet 1. Does it suggest that there are any common factors in this collection? What makes a situation into a drama in newspaper terms?

2] There are probably dozens of different stories that could fit any of these headlines. As a whole class, or in groups, encourage several people to invent stories and tell them to the others. Are they funny or serious? Could the situation seem funny to other people and, at the same time, be quite serious to the people involved? Consider whether each story contains a very unusual situation, or is it one that could happen to anybody? Should people be made aware of such incidents or is it something very private? If so, what makes it newsworthy?

3] IN GROUPS, if these have not already been formed. Ask each group to choose a situation from one of the stories that could be acted out. Then ask the students to imagine that they are the people in the story and arrange themselves in a tableau or living 'photograph' of the most dramatic moment. They might like to have a quick discussion of why they think that moment is the most dramatic, but should keep it within the group.

When they are ready ask them to show their 'photograph' to someone else in order to see whether they can say what makes it dramatic.

It might also be quite interesting to see if the others can guess which headline was used, although some groups may prefer to announce the title of their 'photograph'. What is most important is to see if other students can pick out the gesture or grouping or whatever it is that makes it most dramatic; it may be that a group will want to alter their 'photograph' after showing it, to make use of their audience's suggestions. Can it be re-grouped to add to its dramatic qualities?

4] In the same, or different, groups ask the students to invent an ordinary situation such as a group of people waiting for a bus. Is it possible to form a group 'photograph' which looks ordinary, and then, by changing it as little as possible, make it look dramatic? What did they have to change?

Ideally someone should take a real photograph of both versions, but at least the group should try to remember all the details of gesture and expression, and the position of all the people in the group. At this stage they can show others their 'photographs' for comments if they wish, but at any rate they should be encouraged to relax, and then pose the dramatic 'photograph' again. Is it still the same? Is it still realistic or has it become exaggerated?

Written Work

Before the results of their experiments are forgotten the students should keep an individual record of all the ingredients of drama which were either seen in their 'photographs' or talked about during their work. Encourage them to make drawings that record the position taken by the people in one of the group 'photographs'. (Matchstick or cartoon figures will do.) Ask them to write headlines to match their pictures, using either the word 'drama' or 'dramatic'. If real photographs were taken you might like to fit some of their headlines to the prints at a later stage.

Follow-up Work

Ask the students to look out for further pieces of news reporting which contain theatrical words such as 'tragedy', 'comedy', 'farce', 'plot', 'scene', 'characters', 'melodramatic'. They may be able to compile a list of theatrical terms in everyday use by looking up the meaning of these words in a dictionary. There may be other words or phrases they can find, or think of, which have come from the theatre into various forms of journalism. Radio or television reporting may even suggest phrases such as 'the theatre of war' or 'a pageant of history'.

As further follow-up to the work suggested for the students' own research the teacher may be able to take a short video recording of an educational programme, a pop video, or extract from a television play and to do a breakdown of the number of scenes – not camera shots but real scenes – by which the necessary information is conveyed. How many of the scenes involve such things as car journeys, street scenes, car chases or other mechanical contrivances which may not be appropriate to student drama? The video may be shown in class which means that it can be 'frozen' at certain stages, or it may be a more generalised piece of investigation to be carried out at home.

LESSON 2

Constructing a Story

Every play is concerned to tell some kind of story, not by means of written words and printed pictures, but in living, moving and audible scenes. The theatre does not present real life, it shows us a selection of events, which may seem real, but have been chosen for a particular reason.

Real life, when reported to other people is no longer real. Newsreel film is edited before it is shown and in most cases, even before editing takes place the camera operator and journalist have already selected the events they wish to show.

The practical work which follows is set up in such a way that it concentrates on selection. Students are asked to select and present certain scenes that have a significance for the story they wish to tell. The material is not seen as the most important element of the lesson; it is technique that is important. They will need to be made aware of what they are trying to achieve, and the relevance of the word 'scene' to the work in hand.

Preparation

No special preparation is required for this lesson, apart from the provision of writing materials.

Practical Work

1 IN PAIRS. For convenience, one member is A and the other, B. Allow students a few moments for each one to think of something they have done recently. Emphasise that it must be something real and that they will have to answer questions about it. (Already the process of selection is operating.) Let each person tell the other what they did, in a few words, and then get them to ask each other questions. They may choose whether to chat at random or whether they wish to interview each other in a more formal way. The important thing is that each student needs to build up a complete picture of the background, people and action in the situation.

2 When A is satisfied with B's story, it can be checked out by selecting one scene and directing B to walk it through. The activity might go something like this... 'The door was on this side, right? And you were sitting ... where?' In this way the action will be reconstructed as if it was happening again.

Get them to change over when they reach the end of the scene, remembering that it is only one scene that they have chosen. Ask B to repeat the method on A's scene. It may be necessary to emphasise that no-one is being asked to perform the scene; they are simply going over what happened, where it happened and the relationship between the various incidents and characters in the situation.

3 As each pair finishes, ask them to discuss how they could show the scenes they have walked through to other people. Then, when they are ready, let A demonstrate B's story by telling it to the others. It might sound something like this... 'Susie went to her aunt's house. She had promised to help make biscuits for a jumble sale...'. As A narrates the story, B makes an entrance and goes through the moves. A describes the place and can call on others in the group to stand in for other characters in the story. 'Susie's aunt is called Mary. She is tall and thin and very friendly... She mixes the dough with her hands, not a spoon...'. The narrator is the only one to speak and can direct the whole scene whilst telling the story, without rehearsing it beforehand.

There may not be time to go through all the stories in this way. It might be possible to work in groups of four or six rather than showing to the entire class, but the disadvantage of this is that the teacher cannot lead the necessary discussion with the person whose story is being narrated. It is important to find out whether the representation was accurate, and to analyse exactly what the scene showed. Was it the whole story? Was it the end of the whole episode, the beginning, the climax or an incident that was chosen to be typical of other incidents? Were characters more important than action? Was the story unusual or surprising or did it confirm something that everyone has experienced at some time or another?

N.B. If the class finds difficulty with the techniques involved in this exercise it would perhaps be easier if the teacher demonstrated first, taking a student's story, such as: 'I went skating on Saturday, for the first time...' and showing how the questioning and walking-through might be done. After this the class may be able to get on better, without interruption. There are also other benefits to be gained by the teacher proving that narrative improvisation is something that needs no special acting skills, but may be achieved in a spirit of enquiry.

Written Work

Ask the students to make some kind of a record of one of the scenes. This could be in a very abbreviated form such as a list, or the answers to a questionnaire framed by the teacher. Each record should contain at least the following:
1 the title;
2 the setting;

3 the characters (with a brief description);
4 a brief outline of the events; and
5 the mood (comedy, tragedy, domestic drama, etc.).

If the students wish, they could write out some of it as if it were an extract from a play, in which case they would include stage directions and dialogue, or they could carry out the whole exercise as if it were the 'blurb' for a printed text of the play, and, using some of the vocabulary of dramatic terms they have already acquired, write a paragraph intended to describe the play on the back cover, or for the publisher's catalogue.

A less literate, but keen, group may wish merely to add a scene plan to their list of constituents of the drama.

Follow-up Work

More imaginative story-telling may be undertaken, using the same methods as before but trying to make improbable stories obey the same rules of behaviour and first-person narrative. Students may then take their stories a stage further by having each character in the story narrate the action and report their own speech in turn. Thus, in the original example, Aunt Mary would introduce herself and say 'I am making biscuits for the sale of work. I use my hands to make the dough...', etc. Meanwhile another narrator tells the audience what she is thinking while speaking, for instance 'I am tired and I should like a cup of tea.'

LESSON 3

Narrative Theatre

Simple story-telling in the theatre is a matter of putting together a sequence of scenes to tell a story. Some of these scenes may be very short. Some may well show action. Some may use words to move the story on.

Preparation

> RESOURCE SHEETS 2–6A
> Optional:
> Tape or cassette recorders

Each student will need a copy of resource sheets 2–2A and 3–3A. An impatient or experienced group may wish to tackle the narrative play without help from the teacher, but if time is short and reading dialogue at sight is a problem, the teacher may be able to direct some students through *The Poor Peasant and the Cow* with the rest of the group watching. Although the play is based on a simple story, nevertheless the style is unusual and may well need a good deal of explanation. Narrative theatre is less familiar to Western audiences than to those in the East.

Practical Work

1 The playscript demands four speaking, and one non-speaking role. Either in self-sufficient groups, or in a single group with the rest of the class observing, read the play through aloud. The text itself is not to be taken too seriously, but the method of telling the story should be analysed. At what point do characters speak directly to the audience and when are they simply describing their actions or feelings aloud? Notice should be taken of the absence of any break between what is spoken to other characters and what is spoken presumably to the audience or as an aside. Stage directions are, for the most part, non-existent or part of the words spoken by the characters. Students may wish to discuss the effect that this has on the style of presentation. Does it imply an absence of scenery?

2 Allow the students to try out the scene, with movement. They may wish to appoint a director or they may want to work it out for themselves. Ask them to make sure that they know where they want the audience to be. Even if they do not show the piece, it is important to know where they will address their remarks. It is not necessary to do the whole piece. The style is all that is important.

3 As soon as the students have practised sufficiently, turn to the second story, *The Night the World Ended*. It has not yet been dramatised. Try reading this story in the same way, as a piece of narrative theatre, working either in groups or with the teacher. Some of the story is already in direct speech so the characters have some lines to say. Some of the story is in action, some is merely descriptive. It should be possible for the students to have a go at this without help, even if they concentrate only on the first few paragraphs. In order to get the most from this story they may need to leave out some of the words, or add extra lines for some of the characters. Certain descriptive passages may need to be turned into dialogue or stage directions.

Written Work

Ask the class to try turning a piece of serious reporting from a book, magazine or newspaper into narrative theatre. They may choose their own passage, in which case they should include a copy of the original for comparison, or the teacher may wish to select the passage for them. Ask them to try it as an experiment to see whether it can remain serious. They may also wish to try their hands at writing or taping the opening lines of a scene where someone is defusing a dangerous home-made bomb. It is vital to the situation that the character relays every move and describes everything that can be seen. The students could be given the first line: 'I am approaching the device by crawling towards it. . .'.

Follow-up Work

A short account of the work of Bertold Brecht and some further examples of narrative theatre are given on resource sheets 4–6A. Students may read these and discuss the scenes, particularly the passage from *The Caucasian Chalk Circle* which implies rather than states information about the characters' situation and attitudes. At a simpler level they may prefer to try their hand at creating a fuller version of one of their own stories as a radio play. This is often a good way of finding out how much narrative is needed to tell a dramatic story as economically as possible. The play could be improvised directly into a tape recorder and could be treated as part of an imaginary radio serial or soap opera.

LESSON 4

The Details of a Story

In creating a dramatic story it is important to make all the elements fit into an artistic whole. In real life people may behave inconsistently and the reasons behind their actions may never be known. In the theatre the audience expects to know why something is happening, as well as where, when, and to whom.

Students who find a great deal of excitement in their ability to improvise may become over-inventive, which may put undue stress on others in the scene, or make the drama impossible to take seriously. Even without this necessity for a logical approach, a group should be helped to analyse the who, what, when, and where of a dramatic scene.

Preparation

```
RESOURCE SHEETS 7–7A
Paper and pencils
Optional:
Tape recorder
```

One copy of resource sheets 7–7A will be needed for each group of four in the class. Rough paper and pencils are required for making lists.

Practical Work

 Divide the class into four groups. Ask one group to make a written list of six places, as widely different as possible. The next group makes up a list of six times, varying from times of day to times of year. The third and fourth groups each produce a list of six types of people.

 The teacher puts these lists together so that there are four categories laid out as in this example:

Place	Time	First person	Second person
Cathedral	Morning	Caretaker	Magician
Kitchen	Halloween	Queen	Parent

 N.B. It is perfectly possible to compile these lists beforehand, but it takes away some of the fun.

IN PAIRS. Allocate a category of circumstances from the list to each pair and ask them to make up a scene that explains why those people meet in that place at that time. What do they want from each other?

 If they wish, these scenes, or some of them, may be tried out on the rest of the group. It should be emphasised that this is being done in order that the audience may be questioned at the end as to who the people are, why they met in that place at that time and the means by which that information was conveyed.

 Resource sheets 7–7A contain some photographs. Ask each pair to join with another pair so that they become a group of four whilst still retaining their original partners. One of each pair chooses a different character from one picture to represent. Their partners are journalists who are going to interview them for a newspaper. Before they conduct the interviews make sure that the whole group has discussed and agreed about what is happening in their chosen picture.

6 When they are ready let the journalists conduct their interviews, all at the same time. Give them a time limit and tell them that they should be trying to find out why their partner's character was in that place at that time. They should also be asked to judge what sort of people they are interviewing and whether they respond readily to questioning.

7 At a given signal the journalists should change over to interview the other character in their group. Does this throw any further light on the situation? Are there contradictions?

8 If there is time, the journalists and the characters can compare notes in order to fit all the information together. If there are irreconcilable differences the teacher may have to arbitrate, or the members of the group may have to choose which story to accept. They could also act out the situation, concentrating on showing why the incidents they have been discussing came about.

Written Work

The students may either write a very short account of their group's story, with quotations from either or both the interviews; or they could write a letter as one of the characters describing both the incident and the interview with the journalist, in which case the attitude of the character towards the interviewer will also be important.

Follow-up Work

Using a tape or cassette recorder the interviews could be made into a 'live, on-the-spot' report of the incident.

Students could also be asked to look at a television newscast in order to try to analyse the way interviews amplify the visual or the action in a story. They may also pick out the amount of commentary that is used and decide why it was necesary. The news item may be videoed by the teacher to play in class, in which case students may be able to discuss the means by which they were made aware of the reasons why someone behaved as they did, as well as who and where they were.

LESSON 5

Selecting the Scene

The old-fashioned words 'wheelwright' and 'shipwright' describe trades; similarly the word 'playwright' was used because writing plays was seen as a craft designed to fulfil a certain purpose, produce a certain effect. In the West, however, the writing of plays has come over four centuries or so to be regarded as a literary activity rather than a trade with rules. Yet drama is usually intended to be seen and heard rather than read. The way a playwright structures, or crafts, a play to determine what the audience sees, as opposed to what it is told, fundamentally affect the story's emphasis and meaning on stage.

Lesson 5 is based on an understanding of the principles of dramaturgy laid down by Aristotle. It needs a small amount of theatre history.

Preparation

RESOURCE SHEETS 8–10A

Resource sheet 8 on the Greek theatre may be used to introduce 'dramatic unity' to the group. The teacher could commence this lesson with no more than a very brief outline of the ideas contained in this resource sheet. It is also possible that the material could form the basis of some follow-up work on the Greek theatre. Students will, however, require resource sheet 9, one copy per group. They may need to have this read to them and to be offered an opportunity for discussion of the contents before working on it (see Practical Work 3).

Practical Work

1 After the preliminary introduction, the class should be divided into groups of a convenient number, but not less than four. Ask them to imagine an occasion for a family reunion. It could, for example, be a funeral. They should imagine that one member of the family is missing for some reason and then make up and rehearse as short a scene as possible to show what every other character feels about that missing person. These scenes should concentrate on the missing person; they should not ramble off into details of the meal, the house, or the relationships between other characters.

2 When the scenes have been roughed out, ask the groups to show them to each other. The audience should be questioned as to the information they have received about the missing character during the course of the scene. The questions may include such things as: Did the choice of situation give enough information? Were relationships clear? Were there things in the scene that could have been left out? Were there things that should have been included to make the situation clearer?

The teacher should make sure that there is a direction to the questioning and that the students are not led into making value judgements about the skill, or otherwise, of the performers.

3 The teacher should now either read the newspaper report from resource sheet 9, or copies should be given to the groups. The story describes an episode of extreme and unusual violence. There will need to be some reminder of the principles of Greek theatre with regard to the showing of violent action on the stage. How is it possible to choose one scene that could summarise the whole story? Will this scene be at the beginning of the story, even before the reported incidents? Or will it come at the end, after all the action is over? Will the scenes show the reasons for the violence or the effects of that violence?

At this point it is the discussion which is more valuable than the acting out of the scenes. It may, however, be important to the students that they work on the material for a little longer and put their ideas into practice.

4 The lesson should include time for a general pulling together of ideas. Is there a general consensus of opinion that Aristotle's ideas can be effective? As performers do they need the release of violent action? As audience can they see the effectiveness of choosing cause and effect rather than the action itself? What is the effect of selecting one crucial scene rather than telling the whole story in a number of scenes?

Written Work

Students should find some way of recording one scene from this lesson and of deciding how they would fit that scene into a whole play. They should decide whether to go further back in time, add to the scene to make it longer, or continue beyond the end of the scene. There are various ways to do this; it could be in the form of an essay, as notes, as a cartoon story with significant captions or in dialogue. At this stage the teacher may decide to ask students to work on the Unit 1 student assessment form.

Follow-up Work

Resource sheets 10–10A contain an extract from the opening scene of *The Price* by Arthur Miller. The class may wish to discuss or make notes on the way the playwright lets the audience into the life story of the characters very gradually.

A study of *An Inspector Calls* by J. B. Priestley may reveal a good deal about how a dramatist uses Aristotle's ideas. At this stage the group may be interested in proceeding with a study of conditions in the Greek theatre, and how the Classical dramatists avoided violent action on the stage whilst still creating plays of a very violent nature.

At the end of this unit, students and teachers will need to look back at what has been achieved. If drama is to be seen as more than a random succession of lessons, however successful, then a record of progress is vital. Students' folders or diaries are one way of achieving this, but the student assessment forms included in the resource material at the end of each unit should serve as a basis for a more formal and analytical record of achievement.

RESOURCE SHEET 1

Hostage seized by gun gang in robbery drama

£50m LONDON KIDNAP DRAMA...

FAMILY IN RUNAWAY CAR DRAMA

BABY'S DEADLY ORDEAL – DRAMATIC PICTURE

Blaze drama as mum jumps for her life

MAN HELD IN DRAMA AT PALACE

Real-life drama on the wards

RESOURCE SHEET 2

The Poor Peasant and the Cow

Characters

The Poor Peasant
The Peasant's Wife
The Cowherd
The Judge
The Carpenter (non-speaking)
The Calf and Buttercup (imaginary characters)

PEASANT   There once was a village in which only rich peasants lived...

WIFE   all except one...

PEASANT   and he was so poor that he didn't even have a cow, or any money to buy one...

WIFE   and he and his wife did so wish to have a cow of their very own.

PEASANT   One day the Poor Peasant said to his wife, I have had an idea. Your cousin the carpenter can make us a little calf out of wood, and shape it...

WIFE   and plane it...

PEASANT   and paint it brown, so that it looks like any other...

WIFE   and in time it will surely grow...

BOTH   and be a cow.

WIFE   So their cousin the carpenter shaped the calf...

PEASANT   and planed it...

WIFE   and painted it brown...

PEASANT   and made it with its head hanging down as if it were eating.

COWHERD   The next morning the cows were being driven out to pasture.

PEASANT   Good morning, cowherd. I wonder if you could take my little calf here, out to the pasture? She's so small she can't walk by herself, so you'll have to carry her.

COWHERD   Oh, alright. Heavy little devil, ain't she? Have no fear, I'll watch over her well. So the cowherd took the calf out into the pasture and set her down in the grass. There you are you funny little thing. That's right, eat up. Just look at you eating! Soon you'll be so big and strong that you'll be running round with the rest of the cows. That's right, eat.

RESOURCE SHEET 2A

PEASANT   Soon night came.
COWHERD   All right, girls, time to go home. Come on, we're going home. You too baby, we're going home. No pushing there – we're all going together. Stop eating for a minute can't you. This is what we call dark and it's time to go home. Look, we're going without you. We are leaving. Goodbye. So long. Bye bye.
PEASANT   But the Poor Peasant was waiting anxiously at his door. Good evening.
COWHERD   Evening.
PEASANT   Hey! Where's my calf?
COWHERD   She's still in the meadow, eating.
PEASANT   But it's dark out there. Something might have happened to her.
COWHERD   She wouldn't stop eating.
PEASANT   So they went back to the pasture together, but when they arrived the calf was gone. Someone had stolen it. I must have my calf back.
COWHERD   This is terrible.
PEASANT   That was the only animal I possessed.
COWHERD   But I've never lost an animal in my whole life.
PEASANT   We'll see about that. We're going to the judge. Your Honour, I had a baby calf and this man took it out to pasture and left it, and now it's gone.
COWHERD   Well that's true, your Worship, but I thought she needed to eat some more.
JUDGE   You must give the Poor Peasant a cow in return for the calf which you lost.
PEASANT   Thank you, your Honour.
COWHERD   Goodbye, Buttercup. I'm sorry it has to be you. No, I don't understand it either.
PEASANT   So the Poor Peasant and his wife finally got...
PEASANT AND WIFE   the cow...
PEASANT   which they had so long desired.

(abridged) PAUL SILLS

The Night the World Ended

It was appropriate that two so interested in the After Life as Auntie Florrie and I should be together on the night the world ended. It happened one Friday in the war while mother was shopping at the Co-op. Auntie Florrie was upstairs in the lavatory, Grandma was having a bath, and I had just begun to write my first story in a penny exercise book when a tremendous explosion shook the house and made the ground tremble.

"Zeppelins, Auntie," I shouted, rushing into the passage. "Zeppelins, Grandma! Are you all right?"

Auntie shouted down. "I'm all right. Seems to me like the end of the world's come."

A gust of the supernatural hit me and I shouted up again. "Come on, Auntie. Come on down, Grandma, and don't talk silly. Mother wouldn't go out shopping if it was."

"I'm coming as quick as I can," Auntie answered. "You stay right where you are in case there's anything more."

"If it's the end of the world they don't need any more," I shouted, always most angry when I was most frightened. "What on earth are you doing up there?"

For answer there was another alarming crash as Grandma, trying to get dried and dressed quickly, fell on the bathroom floor. She thought this was a Zeppelin attack on her personally and cried out for Aunt Florrie.

"Lairdsakes," said Aunt Florrie darting to her aid. Without waiting for them any more I opened the front door, for the street was full of the sound of rushing feet.

The whole world at the street end was aflame. A great sheet of fire hung in the sky, lighting up frightened faces of the people running towards it.

"What's up? What is it?" I screamed at them.

They did not wait to talk. They pointed to the flame which stood like judgment in the sky.

"Wells'!" they shouted. "Wells'!"

Wells' was an explosive factory just across the railway line. It consisted of a lot of tin sheds dotted along the edge of a golf course. It can't be Wells', I thought, it's much too big.

My aunt joined me, holding me firmly by the collar as though I were a dog that might bolt.

Grandma, still shaken and complaining, followed her, clutching the door in case another one went off.

"They say it's Wells'. I don't believe it," I shouted.

"Just look at that," my aunt said calmly, joining the people who were staring rapt at the beautiful and immense aurora over heaven. "**It may be Wells', but personally, honey, I'd say a prayer right away. I wouldn't put it beyond God to put an end to this wicked world at any time.**"

My aunt's calm consideration of the matter was as infuriating as it was frightening. God just would not let the world end while Mother and Marjorie were at the Co-op.

"Mother!" I said to Auntie, thinking suddenly that Mother might be in it. "**And Kenneth?**"

"God will look after them," Auntie said.

"Not if He's ending the world," I said.

Mrs Barratt who lived down the road and whose son Bertie went to school with me, collapsed moaning at our gate. Aunt supported her while I went for a chair and a glass of water.

"**My son Teddy, my son Teddy,**" she lamented when she came to. "**He's at Wells' tonight.**"

"**God will watch over him,**" said Auntie, rosy with confidence. "**Just pray.**"

"**My poor Teddy, I'm sure he's gone,**" the old lady wept. "**I know I'll never see him again.**"

I knew Teddy, and had played cricket with him, and I wept too, but I was sure Mrs Barratt was unreasonable in being so certain that he was dead.

"**It isn't Wells'. I'll bet it's Woolwich Arsenal,**" I said, but as I took her arm and helped her across to her home she kept murmuring broken-heartedly, ignoring all my assurances, "**My poor Teddy, my poor little Teddy.**"

As there seemed to no immediate likelihood of a repetition of the disaster, Aunt Florrie gave me permission to run down to the main street to meet Mother. I ran through streets crowded with people watching the eastern light and assuring each other that it was Woolwich Arsenal with the certainty that a short while ago they had been saying it was Wells'. I passed a gesticulating old gentleman with a prophetic white beard and silver hair bearing a paper banner inscribed "**Repent, for the Kingdom of God is at hand.**"

"**The end of the world has come!**" he was shouting and the crowds went hushed and respectful as he passed. "**It's the end of the world,**" he cried. "**Repent! Repent!**" We all thought suddenly of our unforgiven sins.

I fell happily and excitedly on my mother, brother, and sister when I found them. God had spared them after all: God had looked after us.

The Living Hedge, LESLIE PAUL

RESOURCE SHEET 4

BERTOLD BRECHT (1898–1956)

The foundations of modern narrative theatre lie in the work of a German writer, Bertold Brecht. He spent several years as a refugee in America before settling in East Germany in 1949, where he founded the *Berliner Ensemble*.

Brecht felt that the theatre audiences of his time were being insulted, that they were 'asked to leave their brains in the cloakroom'. Most actors relied on an over-emotional, romantic style of performance and those who received training were taught that they should give most emphasis to showing 'real' feelings on stage. Brecht wanted his audience to understand why such feelings came about, and to apply this new understanding to everyday life. If they saw misery portrayed on stage Brecht wanted the people watching to say to themselves: 'That must be how everyone feels who is downtrodden or badly treated. What can we do to stop such things?'

This kind of audience involvement was produced by concentrating on telling a story and showing why the events happened. The style of drama is usually called epic theatre. An epic play is not one in which the action is set thousands of years ago, with whole armies in the cast; the term 'epic' was used by Aristotle (see resource sheet 8) to describe a play which told a story using several episodes, a great many characters and a variety of places and times. Aristotle used the term 'dramatic' to describe the opposite of epic drama, a play which presented a single event, taking place in a single place in a single day.

Epic theatre does not need much scenery. It can, however, employ slides, placards, film, songs and masks if they are necessary to help the story.

Young people's drama is often epic in style. Plays in the classroom nearly always use other methods than those of the traditional theatre; the use of 'role play' rather than 'character-building' is one example of the way we explore these techniques. Sometimes this is because we do not have the time or the resources for any other kind of theatrical method. Often we use epic style because of the need to simplify a play in order to tell an important story to the audience.

RESOURCE SHEET 5

The Caucasian Chalk Circle

Characters
Simon A young man
Grusha A young woman

SIMON   (*formally*) A good morning to the young lady. I hope she is well.

GRUSHA   (*getting up gaily and bowing low*) A good morning to the soldier. God be thanked he has returned in good health.

SIMON   How are things here? Was the winter bearable? The neighbour considerate?

GRUSHA   The winter was a trifle rough, the neighbour as usual, Simon.

SIMON   May one ask if a certain person still dips her toes in the water when rinsing the linen?

GRUSHA   The answer is no. Because of the eyes in the bushes.

SIMON   The young lady is speaking of soldiers. Here stands a paymaster.

GRUSHA   A job worth twenty piasters?

SIMON   And lodgings.

GRUSHA   (*with tears in her eyes*) Behind the barracks under the date trees.

SIMON   Yes, there. A certain person has kept her eyes open.

GRUSHA   She has, Simon.

SIMON   And has not forgotten? (GRUSHA *shakes her head.*) So the door is still on its hinges as they say? (GRUSHA *looks at him in silence and shakes her head again.*) What's this? Is anything not as it should be?

GRUSHA   Something has happened.

SIMON   What can have happened?

GRUSHA   For one thing, I knocked an Ironshirt down.

SIMON   Grusha Vashnadze must have had her reasons for that.

GRUSHA   Simon Shashava, I am no longer called what I used to be called.

SIMON   (*after a pause*) I do not understand.

GRUSHA   When do women change their names, Simon? Let me explain. Nothing stands between us. Everything is just as it was. You must believe that.

SIMON   Nothing stands between us and yet there's something?

GRUSHA   How can I explain it so fast and with the stream between us? Couldn't you cross the bridge there?

SIMON   Maybe it's no longer necessary.

GRUSHA   It is very necessary. Come over on this side, Simon. Quick!

SIMON   Does the young lady wish to say someone has come too late? GRUSHA *looks up at him in despair, her face streaming with tears.* SIMON *stares before him. He picks up a piece of wood and starts cutting it.*

BERTOLD BRECHT

RESOURCE SHEET 6

Time To Go Home

Characters
Stage Manager
First Actor
Second Actor

STAGE MANAGER (*coming through the curtain and addressing the audience*) Ladies and gentlemen. (*louder*) Ladies and gentlemen ... We are very sorry to have to announce that owing to the indisposition of Miss Grant and Mr Barlowe, tonights performance of 'The Temptress' will not take place. Your ticket-money will ... (*more quietly*) It's so unfair! I'm sorry (*looking back*) but I hate being sent out here like this. I'm the stage manager, not the company manager, and it's not my job to tell lies to the audience. (*confidentially*) They are lies you know. They're not indisposed, they're just not speaking. Not to each other, not to the rest of the company, and especially not to you.

We're quite willing to do the show, but no! They won't let it go on without them, so, I'm sorry, you can either change your tickets for another night, and hope they've stopped sulking, or you can ask for your money back (*a light dawns*), or ... the rest of us will ... (*excitedly*) Would you stay? We could still do a play. Not 'The Temptress', that's terrible rubbish anyway, but there's an old play we do sometimes on tour. It's so old no-one remembers who wrote it, but it's beautiful and funny and sad and we could perform it for you now. We wouldn't need scenery or fancy costumes. I'll just open the curtains and if you stay in your seats we'll begin.

(*The stage manager goes off and the curtains open on a stage with pieces of the scenery for 'The Temptress', shafts of overhead light and looped curtains. Two actors come on: one carries a stool and a basket and the other brings some pieces of blanket. The stage manager returns.*)

STAGE MANAGER You see. They're only too pleased to entertain you.
1ST ACTOR Of course. I play the father.
2ND ACTOR And I play the mother (*sitting on the stool and arranging one of the blankets to suggest a baby*).
STAGE MANAGER (*to the audience*) but we'll need your help too. Actors have been doing this for years ... asking audiences to help by exercising their imaginations. You've heard the kind of thing ... 'But pardon gentles all, the flat, unrais-ed spirits that have dared on this unworthy scaffold to bring forth ...'. 'Think when we talk of horses that you see them, printing their proud hooves i' the receiving earth.' There may not be horses, but imagine ...

A HODDER AND STOUGHTON MASTER

RESOURCE SHEET 6A

2ND ACTOR   A night powdered with stars.

1ST ACTOR   Frost-stars on the water in the bucket and ice everywhere, that crackles under your boots. (*Tucking a blanket around the shoulders of second actor*) A fine night, but cold for travellers. Specially when they won't let you in.

STAGE MANAGER   (*assuming the role of innkeeper*) I'm sorry, but it's the rule of the house, no gypsies.

(*From a little distance away one can hear singing: quite tuneful and sad. 'Show me the way to go home.'*)

Show me the way to go home,
I'm tired and I want to go to bed.
I had a little drink about an hour ago
And it's gone right to my head.

2ND ACTOR   (*after a pause, resignedly*) Who's to know? I'm a woman with a baby, like any other, this man is my legally married husband. We're without a home over our heads and we're looking for shelter and work to do. We've broken no law, we've offended no-one. What makes us so different from other people?

1ST ACTOR   Listen to the singing. That's what makes the difference. They've got a known address, they pay taxes and insurance and send their kids to school. They have the right to say we can't share a public house with them, because we're not the public.

2ND ACTOR   We don't want the public bar, not with a baby. We just want a roof over our heads on a cold night and something to eat.

(*The singing has changed, it is much rougher and louder. The song is 'Good night ladies'.*)

Good night ladies. Good night ladies.
Good night ladies, it's time to say goodnight.
So merrily we roll along, roll along, roll along,
Merrily we roll along, across the deep blue sea.

1ST ACTOR   Haven't you got a stable or a shed to put us in? A place where you'd put animals like us?

STAGE MANAGER   (*facing off stage in the direction of the singing*) Time gentlemen please. Hurry along home now, if you don't mind, ladies and gents. (*Crossing the stage in front of the actors*) Take down some of these lights would you? Lights out everyone, lights out.

ROSEMARY LINNELL

RESOURCE SHEET 7

24

RESOURCE SHEET 7A

RESOURCE SHEET 8

ARISTOTLE AND THE GREEK THEATRE

During the time of Ancient Greece (5th to 2nd century BC), the playwrights of Athens wrote many of the world's greatest tragedies and comedies which serve as models for other writers even today.

The theatre for which the Greeks wrote was designed on a large, outdoor scale; the whole community would expect to attend and judge a work, often as part of a religious festival.

The purpose of playwrights was to help this audience understand something about themselves. Are great natural disasters perhaps punishments for the activities of men? Why do people behave in certain ways towards one another? The wide scope of such themes and the vast theatre space dictate a bold, expansive style of writing and acting. The story is often extremely violent. The success of such plays was measured by their effect on the audience, who were expected to think and feel differently about their own lives after a visit to the theatre.

A scientist called Aristotle (384–322 BC) wrote about this intended effect on the audience. He called it 'catharsis'. The audience should be deeply emotionally involved in the drama, so that, by sharing in the emotions of those on stage, they may achieve a purification of their own feelings.

Aristotle claimed that theatre could be a power for the good, showing as it does the effect of each character's life on others, especially the effect of great people's actions on ordinary citizens. However, he warned that physical violence on stage could merely provoke emotion without leading to any deeper understanding of its significance; this is why violent actions in Greek plays are usually scripted to take place offstage. He also wrote that tragedy should lie in the progression of a single chain of events leading from good fortune to misfortune, and that this chain should be brought about by an error of choice on the part of the central character. If there is also some hidden reason for this wrong choice – something that the audience knows but the character does not – this, thought Aristotle, made for a stronger sense of tragedy.

We do not have Aristotle's book on comedy. Greek comedy is often very vulgar, but at its best is about human weaknesses in politics as well as social behaviour, much as it is today. The purpose of comedy is to ask the audience to observe human behaviour in a more emotionally detached frame of mind than that demanded by tragedy.

RESOURCE SHEET 9

FIGHT FOR YOUTH FELLED BY A SWORD

BRAIN SURGEONS were fighting last night to save the life of a youth whose skull was split by a blow from a broadsword in an extraordinary fight with people dressed as cavaliers.

The cavaliers – and several Morris dancers – were trapped in a flat after patrons of a nearby pub chased them through the streets of the town in the early hours of New Year's Day.

The crowd outside, which numbered about 60, began throwing bricks and stones at the first-floor flat and eventually broke down a door.

CONTROL

A youth of 18 was among the first of those who burst in. He was felled by a blow from the sword which split his skull and cut his brain, paralysing part of his body.

The first police car to arrive was stoned and damaged. Then reinforcements arrived and police dogs were used to control the crowd.

Several people were injured by punches from the mob.

The youth was taken to hospital in a coma.

Last night several people were still being questioned by detectives. Others have been released pending further enquiries.

A HODDER AND STOUGHTON MASTER

The Price

Characters
Victor Franz, a police sergeant
Esther, his wife

We are in the attic of a Manhattan brownstone soon to be torn down. Police Sergeant VICTOR FRANZ enters in uniform. He halts inside the room, glances about, walks at random a few feet, then comes to a halt. Without expression, yet somehow stilled he looks at his watch, waiting for time to pass. Then his eye falls on the pile of records in front of the phonograph. He raises the lid of the machine, sees a record already on the turntable, cranks, and sets the tone arm on the record. It is a Laughing Record — two men trying unsuccessfully to get out a whole sentence through their wild hysteria.

He smiles. Broader. Chuckles. Then really laughs. It gets into him; he laughs more fully. Now he bends over with laughter, taking an unsteady step as helplessness rises in him.

ESTHER, his wife, enters. His back is to her.

ESTHER What in the world is that?
VICTOR [*surprised*]: Hi! [*He lifts the tone arm, smiling, a little embarrassed.*]
ESTHER Sounded like a party in here!
  [*He gives her a peck.*]
  [*Of the record*]: What *is* that?
VICTOR [*trying not to disapprove openly*] Where'd you get a drink?
ESTHER I told you. I went for my check-up. [*She laughs with a knowing abandonment of good sense.*]
VICTOR Boy, you and that doctor. I thought he told you not to drink.
ESTHER [*laughs*] I had one! One doesn't hurt me. Everything's normal anyway. He sent you his best. [*She looks about.*]
VICTOR Well, that's nice. The dealer's due in a few minutes, if you want to take anything.
ESTHER [*looking about, hesitates*] I don't know if I want it around. It's all so massive...where would we put any of it? That chest is lovely. [*She goes to it.*]

RESOURCE SHEET 10A

VICTOR   That was mine. [*Indicating one across the room.*] The one over there was Walter's. They're a pair.
ESTHER   [*comparing*] Oh ya! Did you get hold of him?
VICTOR   [*rather glances away, as though this had been an issue*]: I called again this morning – he was in consultation.
ESTHER   Was he in the office?
VICTOR   Ya. The nurse went and talked to him for a minute – it doesn't matter. As long as he's notified so I can go ahead.
[*She suppresses comment, picks up a lamp.*]
That's probably real porcelain. Maybe it'd go in the bedroom.
ESTHER   [*putting the lamp down*] Why don't I meet you somewhere? The whole thing depresses me.
VICTOR   Why? It won't take long. Relax. Come on, sit down; the dealer'll be here any minute.
ESTHER   [*sitting on a couch*] There's just something so damned rotten about it. I can't help it; it always was. The whole thing is infuriating.
VICTOR   They tear down old buildings every day in the week, kid.
ESTHER   I know, but it makes you feel a hundred years old. I hate empty rooms. [*She muses.*] What was that screwball's name? – rented the front parlour, remember? – repaired saxophones?
VICTOR   [*smiling*] Oh – Saltzman. [*Extending his hand sideways.*] With the one eye went out that way.
ESTHER   Ya! Every time I came down the stairs, there he was waiting for me! How'd he ever get all those beautiful girls?
VICTOR   [*laughs*] God knows. He must've smelled good. [*She laughs, and he does.*]
ESTHER   And they're probably all dead.
VICTOR   I guess Saltzman would be – he was well along. Although – [*He shakes his head, laughs softly in surprise.*] Jeeze, he wasn't either. I think he was about. . .my age now. Huh!
[*Caught by the impact of time, they stare for a moment in silence.*]

(abridged) ARTHUR MILLER

STUDENT ASSESSMENT (UNIT 1)

This unit was concerned with story-telling in the theatre. In order to assess your progress look back over the work you were asked to do.

1 Did you find the work interesting? Was some of it more interesting than at other times? If so, why was this?

2 Can you now use your skill to tell a story effectively in drama? Could you do this well enough already? What did you learn from this work?

3 Did you find it easy to work in different sized groups? Were some groupings easier than others? If so why was this?

4 Do you think you work better as a story-teller or as a listener? Which do you enjoy most? Did you learn more from watching other people or from doing it yourself?

5 Was the written work useful? Did you enjoy the chance of working away from other people? Which piece of written work was most worthwhile?

Unit 2 What is Theatre?

There is often some reluctance in both students and teachers to accept that drama can be rehearsed and polished. Performance is seen as an unnecessary strain, and repetition as destroying spontaneity.

Drama is a reflection of life, and as such is a useful teaching method, but it can also become an art, and is therefore a means of expression.

Teachers may overcome the tedium of repeating scenes over and over again for public or examination purposes by teaching a certain amount of technique from the start and by using an experimental approach to performance which explores 'what would happen if we did it this way?'.

It is nearly always the play that is directed by one person that is regarded by the students as tedious in rehearsal, but they do need to be strongly motivated to go through the necessary preparation without simply being driven by a director who is also a dictator.

Many examination syllabuses contain a hidden element of technique which is expressed in terms of such things as effective use of space, ability to communicate in movement and speech or the ability to use theatre form effectively.

To avoid a last-minute scramble to find such techniques of presentation it is probably wise to teach them from the beginning of the course, but in such a way that they are integrated into the material of the lesson. For this reason Unit 2 places an emphasis on the craft of the actor, 'the Mystery', as it used to be called. Most students are keen to know 'how it was done' and find pleasure in practising the craft themselves.

Teachers who have had no drama or theatre training need not be unduly worried about this unit. The techniques are, in themselves, very simple; it is the context that gives them importance.

In each case the lessons are interchangeable and may therefore be given in any order. Much depends on the group and their mood. A lively class may need to be soothed or alternatively encouraged to use their energy in action.

LESSON 1

Concentration

The purpose of this lesson must be explained beforehand. Students need to be told that actors have to accept whatever character or situation is offered, and must then find a way of presenting them realistically. The ability to concentrate all one's efforts and block out distractions is essential to an actor.

Preparation

RESOURCE SHEETS 11–12
Chairs in a clear space

One copy of resource sheet 11, *Nineteen Eighty-Four*, is needed for the teacher in the practical work for this lesson.

Practical Work

1 IN PAIRS, sitting on the floor, students look into each other's eyes without laughing. In spite of the simplicity of this exercise it is almost impossible for some students. They may have to try it again, with another partner. After discussion of the problems, if any, try it once more. This time can they, without making faces, project a feeling of hate towards their partner?

2 IN GROUPS of three or four, one is being menaced by the intense gaze of the others. No word is spoken until the victim feels bound to respond to the menace; they then say something, anything to stop the gazing; it may be only one sentence or one word, but the scene is over. Those who have finished should remain silent whilst watching the others, so as not to spoil their work. The discussion afterwards should be in groups, and may lead students to discover what the final line suggested, in terms of the feeling engendered by the intense staring. What situations emerged? If the teacher and the students wish, some of these situations may be shown to the others, without previous explanation. What seems to be the underlying scenario of each one?

3 Students may now play out their own, spoken version of an inquisition or a tribunal. These may be based on the previous scenes or may be set up by the students or the teacher. The victim is questioned by the others on totally unprepared and perhaps irrelevant matters. Each inquisitor asks only one question in turn. The victim must look at the inquisitors all the time. If they do not make eye contact they may be sharply reminded: 'Look at me!'

4 The teacher should read out the extract from resource sheet 11. Could the class set up a situation where the questioning is similar to that in the extract? The questions should be based on statements, with which the victim may, in real life, agree or disagree, such as simple arithmetic. In the drama, however, the victim must always lie. Someone should stand behind the victim with their hands linked and resting on the victim's head, whilst following the interrogators closely with their eyes. If the victim tells the truth, hesitates or does not answer 'correctly', the interrogator may nod for the hands to be pressed down sharply to represent an electric shock. The victim may cry out. There may need to be some discussion before beginning, or the teacher may suggest the first questioning, such as 'do you agree that the world is flat?' to which the response must be 'yes'. If absolutely necessary the teacher may ask all the questions and the victims and shock–givers may simply respond.

Written Work

In order to recognise the importance of eye contact and concentration, students should be asked to record where they had success or difficulty. It is important to analyse whether the fiction made eye contact easier or more difficult. They should also be encouraged to think about the value we put on looking into or away from each other's eyes in situations from real life, in the theatre, or in front of the television camera.

Follow-up Work

Making a direct statement to an audience is an effective way of getting used to looking directly at someone. Students should be encouraged to keep a relaxed but stationary posture, well balanced on both feet, and to introduce themselves in a personal profile whilst looking into the eyes of the audience. As well as listening, the audience may notice repeated mannerisms or lack of contact, of which the actor may be unaware. Can the audience also hold a quiet, unfidgety position and maintain attention?

Asking students to make an audience turn round, by interesting them in some imaginary occupation or topic, is a useful exercise. The audience should be encouraged to turn as soon as their attention is engaged by the actor.

Resource sheet 12, from *The Birthday Party* by Harold Pinter contains a scene of interrogation which could form an interesting exercise in how much and when actors should make eye contact, and when it is most effective to look away.

LESSON 2

Fights

There is no reason why drama lessons should contain scenes of conflict. However, most students relish the idea of some violent action and it is better that they should know how to handle stage fights safely than run the risk of accident and injury. It is particularly important that girls should be given this dramatic opportunity, as they are often not used to the kind of aggressive–looking scuffling where no-one gets hurt.

Real stage fights need careful rehearsing and this provides an opportunity to emphasise the need for rehearsal under any circumstances, with a concentration on technique.

It should be made clear that weapons are not included in this lesson. Foils, swords, even toy guns, are disallowed, for obvious reasons. If some sort of weaponry is to be introduced into a stage play, then someone must be responsible for it's use and safe-keeping. Licences are required for any sort of fire-arms on the stage, even for 'bangs' off stage.

Falls are included in this section and should be rehearsed for their safety value as well as for fun.

Preparation

> RESOURCE SHEETS 13–14
> Optional:
> Powerful torches
> Piercing buzzer or screech
> Tape recordings of battle scenes and space sounds

No resource material is needed for the practical work in this lesson. The room should be cleared of any obstructions. If it is a small room then small groups should work while others watch. Students should be asked to wear loose clothing and soft shoes.

Practical Work

1 IN PAIRS, students should engage in slow-motion boxing. None of the blows makes contact, and the emphasis is on reaction rather than action. The teacher should insist that this is Marquess of Queensbury rules. Each 'blow' should cause the recipient to bend or turn as if it were making contact. After a few moments the teacher should choose one pair who are working effectively and set up an audience around a 'ring'. The audience should respond audibly to what they see as effective blows by 'ooing' or drawing breath or even booing.

Couples may then engage in 'no-holds-barred fights' which should also be staged in slow motion and without contact. The participants may then make as much noise as they please or as the school will tolerate.

2 The physical control of slow-motion fighting is difficult for some students. A faster method is to learn to pull your punches. Let students work in pairs on a sequence of slaps and blows which can be repeated as often as they wish. As long as it is always exactly predictable the fight can be speeded up and the audience will not see that the blows don't connect. It is always the recipient, who does the acting, that makes the scene seem good.

3 Pushing against a pull is another favourite technique. Whilst one student seems to be holding the other one's ear, hair or arm, the victim should push against the aggressor whilst holding on to his or her hands. It should look as though they are trying to remove the hands and are being dragged around the room at the same time. In fact, it is the victim who makes all the running as well as all the agony. Let the aggressor put in some violent noise as well. Holding one's own arm up behind one's back whilst seeming to be twisted round by an invisible force is a good exercise, as is being buffeted by an invisible enemy. Pulling and wrestling fights are very effective fights for women.

4 In all good stage action falling is a necessary technique. Actors should practise putting their knees together and as close to the ground on one side as possible before falling with the weight on the buttocks, or hips and shoulders. In many respects this resembles parachute landing. Fainting is a simple version of this fall. Dying from a wound may require violent and tense writhing beforehand but the fall itself should always be very relaxed. Stumbling, by catching the toe of one foot against the heel of the other whilst walking is also most effective and can be combined in various comedy routines.

5 Mimed weapons are possible but not often very artistic. A ritualistic or danced version of a battle scene may be a good way of handling this problem or someone may have the necessary skill to teach a good fight with swords, quarterstaff or lances. For most scenes in classroom drama the unarmed fight is often the most useful. As a progression from what has been practised so far, the teacher may set up a group situation where a fight breaks out, perhaps at a club. In groups of not more than six, students may stage their own fight scenes and show them to each other. Can the audience decide what the setting is without being told? How many of the techniques can the actors use in one fight?

Written Work

There are many ways to construct written work from a fight sequence. Students may wish to concentrate on the reasons for the fight, the description of the struggle as if in a newspaper report, a review of a professional boxing match, a scene from a play or a description from someone who was involved. The teacher may wish to go back to resource sheet 9 from Unit 1 and re-enact it with the fight scene included. Which is the more satisfactory version, and why?

A comicstrip version of a fight might describe it in very few words but with a good deal of onomatopoea. A collection of comic book fight scenes might make an interesting collage.

Follow-up Work

A space–war battle may provide an interesting control factor for a group of students who find an interest in fights. 'The Force' may be represented by a beam of torch light in a darkened room or by a buzzer sound and it could perhaps be co-ordinated to a tape of space noises. A sound track of any battle may be made first and the fight mimed to the tape.

The two different fights given in resource sheets 13–13A, *Romeo and Juliet* and resource sheet 14, *The Fight of the Year*, may be rehearsed with or without learning the words, in order to work out the sequence of moves. In the original performance of *Romeo and Juliet*, swords were used. What would happen if this fight were staged as though it were provoked by: (a) the Mafia? or (b) a gang of modern youths, perhaps with a fatal flick knife? In the poem, how do the words suggest physical moves? In many television plays and films, fights and killings often seem commonplace. Imagine that in one of the fights you have staged, someone is killed. Ask the students to set up some chairs as that person's coffin. What would people say if they spoke their thoughts aloud, passing the coffin?

In a normal day's or week's television viewing how many fights are noted? Were they necessary to the story? Were they well staged? Were stunt-fighters used or did the actors themselves 'stage' the fighting?

LESSON 3

Body Language

Simple techniques of movement and bodily characterisation are often useful ways to encourage understanding. Many actors find that to assume the stance of a character is the first step to feeling like that person. Other actors do not find it helpful as a first step, and for those people this section is more helpful as an aid to final performance.

Preparation

Copies of resource sheets 15 and 16 will be needed for each student.

```
RESOURCE SHEETS 15–16
Chairs
Optional:
Paper and pencils
Large mirror
```

As in the section on fights the room should be clear of furniture, although chairs, and possibly writing materials will be needed at the end. Because of the emphasis on shape, students should put on sportswear or simple clothes, and a large mirror might be helpful.

Practical Work

1 Students should stand singly, in a space, with weight evenly balanced on both feet. They should be encouraged to feel the spine drawn up towards the ceiling, arms loose and head well poised. Now ask them to walk on the spot, keeping that easy stance. When they feel easy, ask them to stand with their arms hanging back and knees slightly bent. Can they walk like this and still keep it easy? Does this suggest a character? What about age?

The next stage is to sag forward at the waist whilst keeping the knees a little bent, and move with more of a shuffle in the walk. Is this older?

Using resource sheet 15 as a reference, students should then be encouraged to perform their own sequence of the illustrated posture changes, as an ageing process. If a mirror is available they can check their success for themselves. If not they can check each other's ability to convince.

2 Encourage them to choose a stage in the illustrated sequence, adopt it, and then walk about and meet others, introducing themselves in character, chatting to each other and moving on. Before too long ask them to say whether the people they meet are middle-aged, elderly, active, rheumatic, etc., and check the reality of these postures. Do the postures help them to feel the right age? Discuss other physical changes that are common with increasing age. Without allowing caricature, encourage them to demonstrate a limited ability to read a notice or the small print on a form. What does it feel like to have difficulty opening a jam jar or operating a phone, sitting in a chair, or hearing a conversation? Let these things be done practically, not merely talked about.

3 Resource sheet 16, *The Secret Diary of Adrian Mole* may be read here. Then, in twos or threes, let one student represent an elderly person, living alone, who is showing young visitors around his or her home and giving them a cup of tea. There is no sub-text, it is just for information. Set a time limit on the scenes. All they have to do is decide the name of the old person beforehand.

4 The teacher may then call a meeting of the young people to ask what they can tell about the ability of the elderly people that they visited to cope in the future. The students who played the elderly characters should either listen, out of role, or attend the meeting as relatives. The lesson may end with recommendations, or students may go back to their own elderly person, with suggestions for change.

Written Work

Before too long students should be asked to write down their feelings about whether attention to physical characteristics made it easier to accept the roles, either in themselves or in others.

There is also a great opportunity for in-role writing, either as the old person or as a young visitor.

Follow-up Work

It is not necessarily the case that all the stories were of deprivation. Can the students play a scene where the situation is reversed? What conditions might make the young go to the very old for help? Encourage a change of role so that others get an opportunity to play an elderly character. Look at the degree of realism in mimed activities. How necessary is it to the actor to be realistic, and how much more than a token gesture does an audience need?

Finding a stance for other characters may prove rewarding. A list of words describing status which can be shown in posture might prove interesting; for example: 'proud', 'disdainful', 'hurt', 'dejected'. Pin figures could be drawn, or pictures from magazines and papers collected, as a record of how we adopt movement, gesture and eye levels for all of these attitudes. This may well serve as a shorthand vocabulary for subsequent performance.

LESSON 4

Movement, Voice and Ritual

Whereas much of the material in this pack is realistic, nevertheless, in performance a symbolic use of movement or voice may be the most economical way to convey a message. The teacher should make sure that students are introduced to this lesson in terms of the mastery of technique and that they come naturally to the ritual. It may be very difficult for some young people to accept the idea of ritual without embarrassment.

Preparation

> RESOURCE SHEET 17–17A
> Optional:
> Percussion instruments
> UV lamp
> Blackout materials

The exercises require an uncluttered space, and students will need clothes that allow easy movement. Bare feet are better than shoes. If percussion instruments are available then they may be useful but the emphasis is on voice and physical energy so they are not essential. Copies of resource sheets 17–17A, *The Pilgrim's Progress* will be needed for each student. For the follow-up work a UV lamp is suggested. These are quite easy to obtain and are magical in effect. The bulbs take time to warm up and a complete blackout is necessary.

Practical Work

1 The exercise begins with walking. First just walking easily on the spot, then lengthening the stride and moving in and out, avoiding other people, finally changing direction, without changing pace. Suggest that they hum to themselves as they go, timing their breathing to the rhythm of the walk. Ask them to imagine that they are walking along an empty beach, humming to themselves. As they pick up stones and throw them into the sea can they increase and decrease the volume of the hum? Ask them to imagine wading out into the sea, pacing themselves to the depth and pressure of the water.

In groups as large as possible, can they link arms and walk along together, bending forward and back whilst decreasing and increasing the hum? Can they pick up the impetus of the move without knowing who is the leader? Can they stand still and turn this into a wave effect? Has the hum got a tune?

2 Suggest that they form two opposing groups who menace each other by humming and stamping, or stepping towards each other. Ask them to imagine it as a battle of nerves where volume and steps are used as weapons. Does either group retreat at any time? What happens when they meet? Can they maintain eye contact and volume?

3 Ask the students to keep the same two groups to form burial parties. They will have to find a safe and comfortable way of carrying and laying down one of their number. They may imagine that this comes after the battle sequence. Allow time to perfect the method before they perform it. The movement should be performed to another humming sound. How different is that sound? A large amount of physical control is needed to perform this exercise successfully. Can they add the battle and burial sequences together to make a story? At what point, and how, do the dead fall?

4 The teacher could now either read the two excerpts from *The Pilgrim's Progress* aloud, or give copies to the two groups to work on by themselves. Students should not need much help to interpret the scenes, drawing on the methods they have used in the lesson so far. They may wish to use a narrator or musical sound as well as voices and they may wish to use dialogue; however, they should be encouraged to stick to the more abstract mode of the previous work.

Written Work

Students may wish to write, and perform, a lament to the dead. They should also be able to describe the use of ritual and analyse the meaning of the term, in a theatrical sense, after some initial discussion with the teacher and the rest of the group.

Follow-up Work

Re-rehearsing the *Pilgrim's Progress* scenes, using extra facilities, would be a constructive way of increasing commitment to developing drama as an art form. The use of UV light may suggest ways of making unreal effects and movements such as waves and the Celestial City. The presentation may be enhanced by making some simple scenery using fluorescent paper, cloth or paints. Clothing is also effective if it is chosen carefully to show up or disappear in the light. Even without special lighting these scenes may be effectively presented in sound and movement, with or without music.

Students may wish to reconstruct rituals from cultures other than Christianity. Are there stories similar to John Bunyan's that they can find to work on?

LESSON 5

Assuming a Character

This lesson concentrates on the face and is concerned with expressive facial images. In large scale theatre forms the face is not seen in any great detail, but in drama work on a small scale the face is an important feature of any communication.

Preparation

> RESOURCE SHEETS 18–19
> Sheets of blank card
> Felt tip pens
> String and scissors
> Mirror
>
> Optional:
> Single light source
> Tissue paper or foil
> Brown sticky paper tape
> Newspaper/*papier mâché*
> Suitable glue
> Make-up

Students will need to make simple masks for this session and one copy each of resource sheet 18 is required. The masks will merely be representative at first; the materials shown on the equipment list are sufficient. The sides of large cereal cartons are a good source of blank card. All mask work requires the use of a mirror and for the follow-up more than one would be useful. A single light source such as a projector, or spotlight is also useful.

Practical Work

1 The masks in this lesson are made to measure. Students should make their own masks but they may need help from a partner. The method is shown in the pictures on resource sheet 18, figure A(1). After the blank masks are fitted securely, students should look at the mask both off the face, and on, in a mirror. What sort of person does it suggest? Is it possible to associate an attitude with the mask? It may be a blankness or lack of character, or the placing of the features in a certain position may suggest characteristics such as 'slyness', 'humility' or 'command'.

There is bound to be an element of comedy in these images but students may experiment with all sorts of moods.

2 After a period when they walk around getting used to moving in the masks, students should be asked to work in groups, one masked character being questioned by other unmasked students. They take it in turns to put on a mask and answer questions about how they feel, and how they see themselves, by means of gesture or by simple, single words or sentences; 'are you proud?', 'do you like other people?' and so on according to the attitude expressed by the mask. In a small class the teacher may wish to have this questioning done with the masked 'victims' appearing in a spotlight against the wall, since body language and gesture are more important than words.

3 IN GROUPS of about six let the students make a 'sculpture' of their masked figures giving it a theme and a title reflecting the mood of the masks. The 'sculpture' could express an overall mood such as 'imprisonment', or it could emphasise differences in mood and create a tension between characters. Groups should be given a time limit and should show their 'sculptures' without naming them aloud so that others can understand the intended mood by walking around the group. Finally, collect all the titles and compare them.

4 If there is time, the masks are not falling apart and there is enough interest, students could go on to create a 'cartoon', or silent story, perhaps with vocal sound effects, where the masks are seen in simple movement and gesture. The nature of the story should arise out of the mood of the masks themselves. If interest is waning, copies of resource sheet 19 'AB scene' may be given out, and pairs of students, working without masks, may present their version of the scene, which is capable of being interpreted in a number of different settings.

Written Work

There is the opportunity here to write a short, personal description of the masks and what effect they had on style and mood. Have students any suggestions as to how this style might be continued? If they have used the AB scene then they could write in their own stage directions. If not they could be given the sheet and asked to put in stage directions for its possible presentation by two masked characters.

At this stage the teacher may decide to ask students to work on the Unit 2 student assessment form.

Follow-up Work

There is much that can be done with the use of masks and instructions for making more permanent versions may be found on resource sheet 18. Half masks may also be made and used for spoken as well as silent drama.

With a supply of half-used eye-shadow and other donated items of make-up students can experiment with fantasy and character face changes. Stage make-up is expensive and may be reserved for special occasions but some crepe hair, spirit-gum (or Copydex if necessary to avoid sniffing), and a selection of water-based make-up colours are worthwhile adjuncts to the drama room.

What is vital is that these are seen as effective tools for the presentation of ideas, and not as exercises in the craft of mask-making, or stage make-up. A collection of faces, whether from photographs or magazines, is a useful way of getting students to look at the way people present themselves in expression, dress and posture. This can be built up over some time and could offer a visual reference point for future work.

Nineteen Eighty-Four

He did not remember any ending to his interrogation. There was a period of blackness and then the cell, or room, in which he now was had gradually materialized round him. He was almost flat on his back, and unable to move. His body was held down at every essential point. Even the back of his head was gripped in some manner. O'Brien was looking down at him gravely and rather sadly.

More than ever he had the air of a teacher taking pains with a wayward but promising child.

"There is a Party slogan dealing with the control of the past," he said. "Repeat it, if you please." " 'Who controls the past controls the future: who controls the present controls the past,' " repeated Winston obediently.

" 'Who controls the present controls the past,' " said O'Brien, nodding his head with slow approval. "Is it your opinion, Winston, that the past has real existence?"

Again the feeling of helplessness descended upon Winston. His eyes flitted towards the dial. He not only did not know whether "yes" or "no" was the answer that would save him from pain; he did not even know which answer he believed to be the true one.

O'Brien smiled faintly. "You are no metaphysician, Winston," he said. "Until this moment you had never considered what is meant by existence. I will put it more precisely. Does the past exist concretely, in space? Is there somewhere or other a place, a world of solid objects, where the past is still happening?"

"No."

"Then where does the past exist, if at all?"

"In records. It is written down."

"In records. And—?"

"In the mind. In human memories."

"In memory. Very well, then. We, the Party, control all records, and we control all memories. Then we control the past, do we not?"

"But how can you stop people remembering things?" cried Winston, again momentarily forgetting the dial. "It is involuntary. It is outside oneself. How can you control memory? You have not controlled mine!"

O'Brien's manner grew stern again. He laid his hand on the dial.

"On the contrary," he said, "*you* have not controlled it. That is what has brought you here. You are here because you have failed in humility, in self-discipline."

He paused for a few moments, as though to allow what he had been saying to sink in.

"Do you remember," he went on, "writing in your diary, 'Freedom is the freedom to say that two plus two make four'?"

"Yes," said Winston.

O'Brien held up his left hand, its back towards Winston, with the thumb hidden and the four fingers extended.

"How many fingers am I holding up, Winston?"

"Four."

"And if the Party says that it is not four but five – then how many?"

"Four."

The word ended in a gasp of pain. The needle of the dial had shot up to fifty-five. The sweat had sprung out all over Winston's body. The air tore into his lungs and issued again in deep groans which even by clenching his teeth he could not stop. O'Brien watched him, the four fingers still extended. He drew back the lever. This time the pain was only slightly eased.

"How many fingers, Winston?"

"Four."

The needle went up to sixty.

"How many fingers, Winston?"

"Four! Four! What else can I say? Four!"

The needle must have risen again, but he did not look at it. The heavy, stern face and the four fingers filled his vision. The fingers stood up before his eyes like pillars, enormous, blurry and seeming to vibrate, but unmistakably four.

"How many fingers, Winston?"

"Four! Stop it, stop it! How can you go on? Four! Four!"

"How many fingers, Winston?"

"Five! Five! Five!"

"No, Winston, that is no use. You are lying. You still think there are four. How many fingers, please?"

"Four! Five! Four! Anything you like. Only stop it, stop the pain!"

(abridged) GEORGE ORWELL

The Birthday Party

Characters
Goldberg
Stanley

GOLDBERG When did you come to this place?
STANLEY Last year.
GOLDBERG Where did you come from?
STANLEY Somewhere else.
GOLDBERG Why did you come here?
STANLEY My feet hurt!
GOLDBERG Why did you stay?
STANLEY I had a headache!
GOLDBERG Did you take anything for it?
STANLEY Yes.
GOLDBERG What?
STANLEY Fruit salts!
GOLDBERG Enos or Andrews?
STANLEY En— An—
GOLDBERG Did you stir properly? Did they fizz?
STANLEY Now, now, wait, you—
GOLDBERG Did they fizz? Did they fizz or didn't they fizz? You don't know. When did you last have a bath?
STANLEY I have one every—
GOLDBERG Don't lie.

HAROLD PINTER

RESOURCE SHEET 13

Romeo and Juliet

Characters
The Capulet household:
Sampson
Gregory
Tybalt
The Montague household:
Abraham
Balthasar
Benvolio
Citizens
A Prince

PROLOGUE

Two households, both alike in dignity,
   In fair Verona, where we lay our scene,
From ancient grudge break to new mutiny,
   Where civil blood makes civil hands unclean.
From forth the fatal loins of these two foes
   A pair of star-cross'd lovers take their life;
Whose misadventured piteous overthrows
   Do with their death bury their parents' strife.
The fearful passage of their death-mark'd love,
   And the continuance of their parents' rage,
Which, but their children's end, nought could remove.
   Is now the two hours' traffic of our stage;
The which if you with patient ears attend,
What here shall miss, our toil shall strive to mend.

[*Enter* SAMPSON *and* GREGORY, *of the house of Capulet, armed.*]

SAMPSON I strike quickly, being moved.
GREGORY But thou art not quickly moved to strike.
SAMPSON A dog of the house of Montague moves me.
GREGORY The quarrel is between our masters and us their men.
SAMPSON 'Tis all one.
GREGORY Draw thy tool; here comes two of the house of the Montagues.
SAMPSON My naked weapon is out: quarrel, I will back thee.
GREGORY How! turn thy back and run?
SAMPSON Let us take the law of our sides; let them begin.

[*Enter* ABRAHAM *and* BALTHASAR.]

GREGORY I will frown as I pass by, and let them take it as they list.
SAMPSON Nay, as they dare. I will bite my thumb at them; which is a disgrace to them, if they bear it.
ABRAHAM Do you bite your thumb at us, sir?
SAMPSON I do bite my thumb, sir.

RESOURCE SHEET 13A

ABRAHAM Do you bite your thumb at us, sir?
SAMPSON [*Aside to* GREGORY] Is the law of our side, if I say ay?
GREGORY No.
SAMPSON No, sir, I do not bite my thumb at you, sir, but I bite my thumb, sir.
GREGORY Do you quarrel, sir?
ABRAHAM Quarrel, sir! no sir.
SAMPSON If you do, sir, I am for you: I serve as good a man as you.
ABRAHAM No better.
SAMPSON Well, sir.
GREGORY Say "better": here comes one of my master's kinsmen.
SAMPSON Yes, better, sir.
ABRAHAM You lie.
SAMPSON Draw, if you be men. Gregory, remember thy swashing blow.   [*They fight.*

[*Enter* BENVOLIO.]
BENVOLIO Part, fools! you know not what you do.
                         [*Beats down their swords.*

[*Enter* TYBALT.]
TYBALT Turn thee, Benvolio, look upon thy death.
BENVOLIO I do but keep the peace:
TYBALT I hate the word,
As I hate hell, all Montagues, and thee:
Have at thee, coward!   [*They fight.*

[*Enter several of both houses, who join the fray; then enter Citizens, with clubs.*]
CITIZENS Clubs, bills, and partisans! strike! beat them down! Down with the Capulets! down with the Montagues!

[*Enter* PRINCE, *with Attendants.*]
PRINCE Rebellious subjects, enemies to peace,
Profaners of this neighbour-stained steel, –
Will they not hear? What, ho! you men, you beasts,
That quench the fire of your pernicious rage
With purple fountains issuing from your veins,
On pain of torture, from those bloody hands
Throw your mistemper'd weapons to the ground,
And hear the sentence of your moved prince.
Three civil brawls, bred of an airy word,
By thee, old Capulet, and Montague,
Have thrice disturb'd the quiet of our streets,
If ever you disturb our streets again,
Your lives shall pay the forfeit of the peace.
To know our further pleasure in this case,
Once more, on pain of death, all men depart.

(abridged) WILLIAM SHAKESPEARE

The Fight of the Year

'And there goes the bell for the third month
and Winter comes out of its corner looking groggy
Spring leads with a left to the head
followed by a sharp right to the body
    daffodils
    primroses
    crocuses
    snowdrops
    lilacs
    violets
    pussywillow
Winter can't take much more punishment
and Spring shows no signs of tiring
    tadpoles
    squirrels
    baalambs
    badgers
    bunny rabbits
    mad march hares
    horses and hounds
Spring is merciless
Winter won't go the full twelve rounds
    bobtail clouds
    scallywaggy winds
    the sun
    a pavement artist
    in every town
A left to the chin
and Winter's down!
    Tomatoes

    Radish

    Cucumber

    Onions

    Beetroot

    Celery

    And any

    Amount

    of lettuce

    For Dinner.
Winter's out for the count
Spring is the winner!'

ROGER McGOUGH

RESOURCE SHEET 15

Ageing Figures

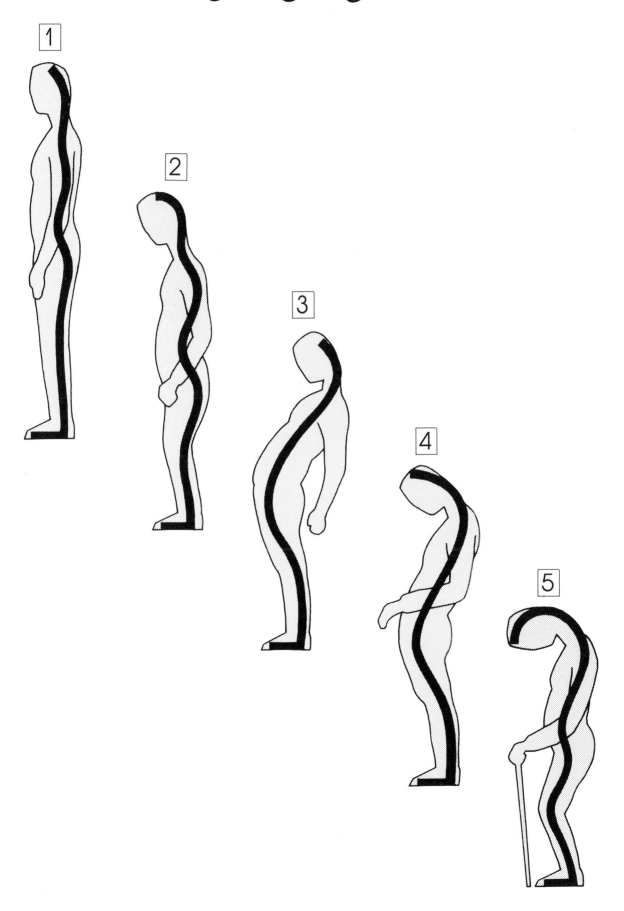

The Secret Diary of ADRIAN MOLE Aged 13¾

Monday January 19th

I have joined a group at school called the Good Samaritans. We go out into the community helping and stuff like that. We miss Maths on Monday afternoons.

Today we had a talk on the sort of things we will be doing. I have been put in the old age pensioners' group. Nigel has got a dead yukky job looking after kids in a playgroup. He is as sick as a parrot.

I can't wait for next Monday. I will get a cassette so I can tape all the old fogies' stories about the war and stuff. I hope I get one with a good memory.

Tuesday January 20th
FULL MOON

The Samaritans met today during break. The old people were shared out. I got an old man called Bert Baxter. He is eighty-nine so I don't suppose I'll have him for long. I'm going round to see him tomorrow. I hope he hasn't got a dog. I'm fed up with dogs. They are either at the vet's or standing in front of the television.

Wednesday January 21st

I went to see old Mr Baxter after tea. My father dropped me off on his way to play badminton. Mr Baxter's house is hard to see from the road. It has got a massive overgrown privet hedge all round it. When I knocked on the door a dog started barking and growling and jumping up at the letterbox. I heard the sound of bottles being knocked over and a man swearing before I ran off. I hope I got the wrong number.

Monday March 16th

Went to school. Found it closed. In my anguish I had forgotten that I am on holiday. Didn't want to go home, so went to see Bert Baxter instead. He said the social worker had been to see him and had promised to get Sabre a new kennel but he can't have a home help. (Bert, not Sabre.)

There must have been a full week's washing up in the sink again. Bert says he saves it for me because I make a good job of it. While I washed up I told Bert about my parents getting a divorce. He said he didn't hold with divorce. He said he was married for thirty-five miserable years so why should anybody else get away with it? He told me that he has got four children and that none of them come to see him. Two of them are in Australia so they can't be blamed, but I think the other two should be ashamed of themselves. Bert showed me a photograph of his dead wife, it was taken in the days before they had plastic surgery. Bert told me that he was a hostler when he got married (a hostler is somebody doing things with horses) and didn't really notice that his wife looked like a horse until he left to work on the railways. I asked him if he would like to see a horse again. He said he would, so I took him to see Blossom.

It took us ages to get there. Bert walks dead slow and he kept having to sit down on garden walls, but we got there eventually. Bert said that Blossom was not a horse, she was a girl pony. He kept patting her and saying 'who's a beauty then, eh?' Then Blossom went for a run about so we sat down on the scrap car, and Bert had a Woodbine and I had a Mars bar. Then we walked back to Bert's house. I went to the shops and bought a packet of Vesta chow mein and a butterscotch Instant Whip for our dinner, so Bert ate a decent meal for once. We watched *Pebble Mill at One*, then Bert showed me his old horse brushes and photographs of the big house where he worked when he was a boy. He said he was made into a communist when he was there, but he fell asleep before he could tell me why.

Came home, nobody was in so I played my Abba records at the higest volume until the deaf woman next door banged on the wall.

Friday June 12th

Had a message from the school to say that Bert Baxter wanted to see me urgently. Went round with Pandora (we are inseparable). Bert is ill. He looked awful, Pandora made his bed up with clean sheets (she didn't seem to mind the smell) and I phoned the doctor. I described Bert's symptoms. Funny breathing, white face, sweating.

We tried to clean the bedroom up a bit, Bert kept saying stupid things that didn't make sense. Pandora said that he was delirious. She held his hand until the doctor came. Dr Patel was quite kind, he said that Bert needed oxygen. He gave me a number to ring for an ambulance, it seemed to take ages to come. I thought about how I had neglected Bert lately and I felt a real rat fink. The ambulancemen took Bert downstairs on a stretcher. They got stuck on the corner of the stairs and knocked a lot of empty beetroot jars over. Pandora and me cleared a path through the rubbish in the downstairs hall and they steered him through. He was wrapped in a big, fluffy red blanket before he went outside. Then they shut him up in the ambulance and he was sirened away. I had a big lump in my throat and my eyes were watering. It must have been caused by the dust.

Bert's house is very dusty.

(abridged) SUE TOWNSEND

RESOURCE SHEET 17

The Pilgrim's Progress

*The following passages have been adapted from this well-known Christian allegory. John Bunyan (1628–1688) is believed to have written **The Pilgrim's Progress** while in prison for unlicensed preaching. He writes as if he saw the events in a dream.*

The fight with Apollyon

But now, in the Valley of Humiliation, Christian was hard put to it for he was met by the foul fiend Apollyon, who taunted and threatened him. He straddled quite over the whole breadth of the way and said, 'Prepare thyself to die, for I swear that here I will spill thy soul'. And with that he threw a flaming dart at Christian who caught it on his shield and drew his sword to fight back.

The battle raged for above half a day, with Apollyon roaring in the voice of a dragon and Christian growing weaker and weaker with the wounds inflicted upon him. Then Apollyon, espying his opportunity, began to gather up close to Christian, and, wrestling with him, gave him a dreadful fall so that his sword flew out of his hand. Then roared Apollyon, 'I am sure of thee now', and would have pressed the life out of him, but that Christian caught his sword again and gave him a deadly thrust, so that he took to his dragon's wings and sped him away, and was seen no more.

Peter Straker as Apollyon, in the Roundhouse production of *Pilgrim*, 1975

Crossing the river

The pilgrims looked across towards the Celestial City. The light that was reflected from its golden walls was so bright that they could not with open face behold it but must cover their eyes. So I saw that as they went on, there met them two men in raiment that shone like gold, also their faces shone as the light. They conducted them within view of the gate to the Celestial City. But when they were there they caught sight of a river that ran betwixt them and the gate. There was no bridge to go over and the river was very deep, but the men said, 'You must go through or you cannot come at the gate'.

The pilgrims began very much to despond in their minds and looked this way and that, but no way could be found in which they could escape the river. Then they asked the men if it were all of one depth, 'No', they said. 'And here we cannot help you because you shall find it deeper or shallower as your belief weakens or is strong.'

As they entered the water so their fears and guilt for past deeds rose up with the waters to overwhelm them. One cried out, 'I sink in deep waters, the billows go over my head, all the waves go over me'. Great darkness fell upon them and apparitions and evil spirits tormented their souls, so that sometimes they would have gone quite down in horror of mind and heart-fears that they should die in that river, but that some more hopeful had much ado to keep them above water. Then they took courage and presently found ground to stand upon; and so it followed that the rest of the river was but shallow. Thus they got over and entered with a host of the Shining Ones into the Celestial City.

RESOURCE SHEET 18

Mask-making

A The basic mask
(made from the front of a cereal packet)

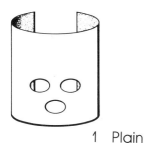 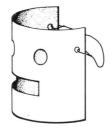 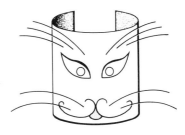

1 Plain

2 Decorated

B Real-face mask

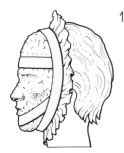

1 Cover face with folded cooking foil. Make breathing holes. Do not keep it on for too long. Tape in place with brown adhesive paper.

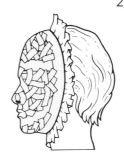

2 Cover foil with smaller pieces of brown sticky paper, until no foil can be seen. Do not cover breathing holes. Foil shape can be removed if face becomes too hot, and replaced for further work.

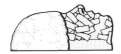

3 Carefully remove mask shape. Fill with crushed newspaper to retain shape and apply layers of *papier-mâché*. A final layer of cheesecloth or gauze soaked in paste will strengthen it.

4 Trim the dried *papier-mâché*. Foil may be removed. Cut eye and mouth holes, and trim nostrils. Seal with shellac and paint.

Holes are cut to correspond with the real position of eyes and mouth.

C Half mask

Make foil mould as above. After removing it from the face, trim it on a line from the top lip to the bottom of the ear. Support it with newspaper and add *papier-mâché* to build up features. Trim, seal and paint as before.

RESOURCE SHEET 19

AB scene

A	What are you doing here?
B	I was walking.
A	Only that?
B	Enjoying the moonlight.
A	What were you doing here?
B	Don't you know?
A	I don't know anything.
B	You sent me the message.

Underground to Canada

There was the scuffling sound of two horses. Julilly knew it was the two men they had seen moments before.

'What do you want of me?' the small driver of the wagon asked clearly in a strong voice.

'We want to know if you've seen four slaves – two men and two girls – along this road tonight.'

'No.' The Quaker didn't hesitate. 'I haven't seen two men and two girls anyplace along this road.'

It's a lie he's tellin', Julilly thought, and then checked herself. He wasn't lying, he had seen two men and two boys running out of the woods. That's what he thought he had in his wagon. Mr Ross was a smart man to have them dress in boys' clothes.

'I don't trust one word you stealin' Abolitionists say.' The man on the horse began talking louder. 'Did you know that the new Fugitive Slave Act, just passed by Congress, lets the slave owners retake human property in any state – north or south.'

'I am well aware of this cruel and unjust act,' the wagon driver replied quietly.

'Unjust, you say.' Now the slave catcher was shouting. 'People like you can be put in jail and fined $1000 for just givin' a fugitive a meal.'

Julilly shuddered. How could they ever escape? They could even be hunted now in the free states of the North.

'We better see what this farmer has in his wagon.' The other horseman finally spoke. 'Get down and turn back the canvas on that wagon!'

Julilly heard their driver jump from his seat to the ground.

'You can see that it's hay I carry to my cousin in the next town.' The Quaker continued to speak softly as he slowly pulled back the canvas from a corner of the wagon.

Julilly gripped Liza's arm. She didn't move, but she did open her eyes. Praise the Lord, it was still dark!

'It is hay.' The second horseman spoke quickly. 'We'd better be ridin' back to the river before daylight breaks.'

They rode away without another word.

The little driver pulled the canvas back over the wagon. He leaned over it.

'When daylight breaks,' he said to the four slaves who lay tense and shaken under the hay, 'we'll stop in a deserted barn along the way and have our breakfast.'

(abridged) BARBARA SMUCKER

RESOURCE SHEET 21

The Smallest Pawns in the Game

And then there was Raïa. She lived at Tours with her mother, her fifteen-year-old sister and her baby brother. Her father had just died. In 1941 the family were summoned to the Police Commissariat where they were each given a yellow star. Only her brother, aged two, was excused this humiliation. Raïa's star had an extraordinary effect on her schoolmates – even those she had known all her short life and whose parents were friendly with hers. Now they simply turned their backs. (Only later did she learn that they did so because their parents were afraid that their children might be arrested with their Jewish friends. The Gestapo were not too particular when it came to details.)

With all the anti-Semitic propaganda and restrictions, the family was reduced to poverty. The curfew kept them at home after six p.m. They lived permanently in fear of their lives. Then came the first deportations; Drancy became a dreaded name and hatred crept into people's hearts.

At six p.m. on 15 July 1942, when the curfew fell, Raïa and her family shut themselves in. Her mother, who was ill, was already in bed when they heard the sound of tramping boots outside. The Gestapo were there. Her mother had to get out of bed to pack a few things, 'just enough for the journey,' said the Gestapo officer. 'You will be given all you need later.' Raïa's mother pleaded, 'I'm ill, please let me stay with my children!' 'They will be going with you,' came the curt answer. And the little family was led outside. Seals were set on the door.

Exactly the same thing was going on one floor above with the family of Raïa's friend, Annie. (Annie's father had already been deported.) The two families were assembled in the street and loaded into a bus. But there was not enough room. 'Wait there,' the Gestapo man ordered. 'We'll be back to fetch you.' So Raïa and her baby brother, thirteen-year-old Annie and her brother, aged nine, were left behind. Raïa continues, 'What could we four children do? I won't go into the screams and the tears and all the rest of it. I will leave you to imagine what a human being, be he father, mother or child, feels in such a situation. When you are a toddler like my brother you are still very dependent on your mother. I thought my little brother would never stop crying.'

So there they were, two teenage girls with their small brothers. 'We were very lightly dressed because of the heat; never before had our parents left us alone; we could not get into the house; we had no money. The instinct of self-preservation made us decide to run for it before they came back to look for us.' But where could they go? The best thing seemed to be to make for the banks of the Loire. So off they went, hugging the walls, trying to hide their yellow stars. 'I had the greatest trouble keeping my brother quiet,' said Raïa. 'He had wet his pants and was crying for Mummy. We were terrified that he would attract attention, so we hid behind a pile of scrap metal.' Annie and Raïa thought of all the non-Jewish people they knew who might help them. Finally they decided to call on a Polish family. But the Poles, terrified at the sight of the children, slammed the door in their faces. So they returned to the river bank and there spent a sleepless night.

A HODDER AND STOUGHTON MASTER

RESOURCE SHEET 21A

As Raïa's little brother refused to leave her side Annie went alone to see the lady at the creamery in Tours where their mothers always went. She returned with a huge omelette and a loaf. And so on, day after day, until the creamery lady found them a *passeur*, a guide. He agreed to take them secretly into unoccupied territory. Disguised as a priest he met them at the bus terminal. The children had no idea where they were going, but when, after driving some way, they saw the priest making ready to get off they knew that they, too, must get off at the next stop. It was only then that Raïa realised that the score of people who got off with them all belonged to the priest's flock. As the bus drove away he explained to them that, to avoid German checkpoints farther on, they had now to walk another thirty kilometres across country.

That walk was pure torture for fourteen-year-old Raïa. She had to carry her small brother all the way. No one else offered to do so – even if they had, he would have refused to leave his sister. After a while he fell asleep, but that only made him feel heavier to Raïa who lagged more and more behind. She caught up only when the others stopped to eat. As they opened their packets of sandwiches the children watched, having nothing to eat themselves, though someone was generous enough to give them half a tomato to share.

Night fell and the *passeur* told them, 'Stick together, for if someone sees us in the distance they'll take us for a tree or a bush.' They moved on and Raïa's torture began again. She had eaten practically nothing and was exhausted. Her sandalled feet, cut by the bristly corn-stubble, were sore and bleeding. Her brother felt heavier and heavier and in the pitch dark she kept on losing contact with the others. By peering ahead into the obscurity she could just discern what looked like a tree moving and she knew it was one of the party. To add to the terrors of that night the alarm was often raised as they passed close to a village. Dogs barked, whistles blew and occasionally a flare rose into the sky. Everyone would then flatten themselves on the ground and Raïa had almost to suffocate her brother to stop him screaming. Yet those terrifying moments were in one way a blessing – they allowed her time to regain her strength.

Finally the *passeur* halted them. 'We are now three hundred metres from the demarcation line,' he told them. 'I have pointed out the road to this young couple. Just follow them.' As soon as he was gone the couple told the children, 'We grown-ups are going to rest a bit here. As your pace is slower than ours you go ahead and we'll catch you up in ten minutes.' And they showed them the direction. The children set off but as after some time there was no sign of the others they retraced their steps to where they had left them. But there was nothing to be seen, save an umbrella that one of the party had forgotten. The children were aghast at having been left in the lurch. Then it struck them. 'We suddenly realised,' Raïa told me, 'that the grown-ups had sent us off on purpose in the wrong direction. They wanted to get rid of us, the weak ones of the party for, who knows, we might have ruined everything at the last moment.'

Not knowing where to go they just walked on and on until at last they saw houses ahead. Help at last! But suddenly every dog in the neighbourhood began barking. 'In a panic,' Raïa said 'we knocked at one door after another, but no one answered. Yet as I knocked I called out, "We are only children so don't be afraid. We are lost . . ." Finally, from behind a door, came a man's voice,

"You are five kilometres from the line. Be careful – a patrol comes this way every two hours. There's nothing I can do to help you."'
So the little ones staggered on until, on the outskirts of the village, they found a barn. There they sank into the hay utterly exhausted. And the barking of the dogs died away.

At dawn next day a farmer appeared and threw them out. All day they lay hidden in the undergrowth by the roadside. Once a German soldier came past on a horse and Raïa trembled. 'Once again I nearly had to suffocate my brother for fear he might cry.' They were all in a sorry state, clothes torn and bodies covered with scratches which drew swarms of flies. They pushed on and Raïa spotted a farm which somehow looked friendly. A young woman welcomed her, sat her and her brother down before two huge bowls of milk. She was so sweet that Raïa poured out her story. The young woman pointed to a house with a red roof. 'It is in the unoccupied zone. You have five kilometres to do without a scrap of cover. You must try it during the midday meal when the Germans are less alert.'

So those two brave, obstinate little girls, Raïa and Annie, with their charges, set off on the last perilous stage of their journey to freedom. Raïa's brother refused to walk – he was too tired. So was she. But he was a piece of baggage she could not abandon. She lifted him up and stumbled on across the rough, parched fields. The midday sun was scorching and she felt a terrible thirst. More and more often she had to stop and rest so that soon she was far behind Annie. Then the famous red roof came closer; she could even make out the house. Annie and her brother were almost there. Watching them Raïa knew she could go no farther. She collapsed and sat there on the ground, her brother beside her, for she knows not how long, unable to make any movement. Raïa thought it was the end. 'From the red-roofed house Annie and her brother were waving. They were saved – I felt I could never make it. I got up slowly, picked up my brother and began walking, but only very slowly. The house seemed a little nearer, when I saw some men on a haystack waving frantically. I don't know how I reached them, for the next thing I knew was people all around me. Someone was washing my feet. They told me that I had crossed the road just behind five German soldiers with two dogs. The peasants were terrified they would devour us.'

The children were safe though Raïa's ordeal was far from ended. She, and her brother clinging to her, were passed on from hand to hand – at fearful risk to themselves and their saviours – until the war ended. It was only then that Raïa heard about the German extermination camps. Until then she had never lost hope of seeing her mother and elder sister again. But the only trace of them that ever reached her was an official paper which said: deported from Tours, 15 July 1942. Died at Auschwitz, 20 July 1942.

Raïa and her brother had escaped a similar fate because there was no room in the Gestapo's bus. Modestly, but with complete truth, Raïa says: 'There's nothing extraordinary about my story. All those who escaped the Nazi man-hunt owe their survival to a variety of miracles.'

(abridged) PETER TOWNSEND

STUDENT ASSESSMENT (UNIT 2)

This unit was concerned with performance skills and effective communication. In answering each question try to give examples from the work you have done.

1 How well do you communicate with an audience? Do you find it easy to make people listen? Do you enjoy using body language and movement?

2 Did you find any of the work particularly hard? Do you enjoy having to work hard?

3 What uses have you found, outside the drama room, for any of these skills?

4 Did you find it easier to do this work alone, or as part of a group? Why do you think this was?

5 Which of the exercises in this unit do you think could do with more work from the group? Are there other skills which you would like to have studied?

Unit 3 Working Creatively as Part of a Group

The work in this unit is concerned with the idea that drama is a social activity. It is true that much of the work in the other units also depended on group work, but this section is aimed at a direct exploration of what it means to be a creative factor within a group. It will be the teacher's task to keep that focus before the student's eyes throughout the work, since so much of the intervening time in any student's life is spent on attaining individual, intellectual development. The object of this unit is to look at the way the individual behaves in a group, and this is structured on two levels: the real interaction of the students, and the subject matter.

Since much of the education which young people receive is based on training the reason and the memory, drama is often seen as a wild release from academic modes of working, rather than a continuation of learning through practical experiment which recognises and encourages emotion. This unit should stimulate sufficient excitement to keep a spirit of creativity going throughout the lesson, and provide enough opportunity for the individual to draw back and consider his or her place in society. Teachers may need to space out the sessions according to the ability of the class to handle group work in a sensitive way. The establishment of a co-operative and trusting class, capable of doing drama together as a whole group, may mean having to do variants of some lessons for several sessions, with further analysis by the group of their own strengths and weaknesses in this respect. Useful trust exercises can be found in *Theatre Games. A New Approach to Drama Training* by Clive Barker (Eyre Methuen, 1977) and in many other drama books available from libraries and educational publishers.

Because of the emphasis on co-operative group work, the idea of performance is less important than it was in earlier units. The students are encouraged to undertake roles in the drama, rather than fully developed characters. There are, however, several opportunities in the follow-up work for teacher and students to develop both themes and resource material to a deeper level of characterisation, or for presentation to an audience.

LESSON 1

Trust

The drama teacher should be prepared to discuss with students what they feel, or understand, at each step of a lesson; this will help to convey the importance of trust between everyone in the group before work begins. It is important at the beginning of this, and every drama lesson, that the skills expected of the students are carefully explained. In this way the assessment procedure and the sense of gained experience – rather than aimless fun – can be arrived at more easily.

Preparation

> RESOURCE SHEETS 20–21B
> Blackout facilities, or material for blindfolds
> Chairs and desks
> Method of making a loud bang

No resource material is needed for the practical work in this lesson. The room should be well set up beforehand since there is a considerable amount of activity. The outside world must be excluded as much as possible to aid concentration. It may not be possible to turn off the intercom but this lesson is unsuitable for a large hall which is a throughway for other people.

It is also important that there is no dangerous or fragile equipment in the room since either the windows will be blacked out, or the students will be blindfolded for part of the time. Chairs, desks or other pieces of movable equipment are necessary. It is essential to be able to make a loud bang at some stage. A cap pistol would be exciting but a wooden block slammed down on another wooden surface would do, and might be more reliable. Some students may be trusted to keep their eyes closed during the exercises, or the teacher may prefer to provide a number of scarves or strips of cloth as blindfolds.

Practical Work

1 IN PAIRS, and in total silence, A leads a 'blinded' B around the room by placing one finger on the tip of B's shoulder. B has to trust A not to allow any collision. The teacher should not be too worried about occasional squeak or laughter at this point. At a given signal B may become sighted again and the pairs can talk to each other about the experience. They should then change over so that B leads A through the experience with, perhaps, a few added risks or a faster pace.

2 The students may now build an obstacle course. It should be discussed when it is finished to make sure that it is suitably difficult, without being dangerous. Working in threes or fours and again in silence, a sighted leader leads a blinded group through the maze. The rules of the game are important in that the leader must use only one finger to touch the members of the team and the team should not hold on to each other. They will, of course, need to feel with their hands as they go along. If there are any members of the group who are genuinely afraid of this exercise, they can still be part of the trust, either by taking on the role of leader or by helping to guide a team out of trouble.

3 At the end of the exercise, and after allowing time to talk about their feelings, the teacher should set up a final exercise which will lead into the piece of drama. In this case the obstacles should be arranged by the class to make it impossible to walk in a clear, straight line from one end of the room to the other. In teams of perhaps four or five they are to plan a route through the obstacles that will get them to the opposite end of the room. After a good look at the 'minefield' they must all, even the leader, be blindfolded or shut their eyes; Alternatively, the lights should be turned out. This time the silence must be made very important as the teams will need to listen out for and avoid other teams going through the same route. As each team makes it to the end they become a silent welcoming party to bring the other teams into safety.

4 At this point the discussion should be led by the teacher. The exercise is bound to have produced moments of near collision, accident or sheer silliness which may need to be talked out, but the teacher should try to lead the conversation from the particular to the general by drawing attention to the success of touch as a means of communication and the sense of reliance on things like hearing other people's breathing or sensing when someone else was near. Was there any sense of panic? What did it feel like to place all your trust on other people? How much do people in a dangerous situation need to depend on a leader? To what extent does the individual need to give up independence for the good of the whole? What makes a good leader in times like this?

These and other questions may be fruitfully introduced at this stage, but it is important that the discussion does not take up more time than the drama.

5 Without too much time elapsing the students should re-play the last exercise as if it were an escape where total silence is essential. Depending on the nature of the class they may want to be a number of prisoners of war, or a band of families trying to cross an unspecified border, or a group of beseiged people on a mission to get supplies back into the city. Either in the same teams as before, or in different teams, let them make the same journey across the room, only within a dramatic context. At this stage there should be no mention of character, only of the situation. To make it seem more real they should be told that the obstacles represent a minefield, or a guarded No Man's Land, and that any untoward sound will force every single person in the room to 'freeze'. They will stay like that until the leader of their own team considers it safe to go on. The teacher, and any other students who may be 'outsiders' for some reason, should assume the role of guards who will take note of any who make unnecessary noise and mark them down for arrest when they reach safety. The teacher may make a sudden loud bang at some point to introduce a feeling of alarm. In this version of the exercise the students should not be blindfolded and the room needs only to be darkened where possible, in order to give atmosphere. To maintain the feeling of trust, any team who finishes should stand by to welcome the others as they come to safety, if possible by taking their hands. In this way everyone remains part of the drama to the end rather than forming an audience of unfriendly 'outsiders'.

6 In the discussion that follows, the question of blaming those who might be arrested should be glossed over, if not totally ignored. Suffice it to say that if one person is singled out, the whole group is in danger. What may be pursued further is the difference between the real dependence of team members on each other and on their leaders in the earlier exercises, and the acted dependence of the drama, in which the students' real experience was used to bring to life a fictional situation. Did the students recognise any of their real feelings in the dramatic situation? Were they able to make the drama as convincing as the reality? Was it more, or less satisfactory than the real situation?

Written Work

Students should be able to put down how they rate the qualities of leadership and their own feelings of trust in relation to the work that they have done. It may be useful for the teacher to propose some questions, such as what was pleasant about entrusting oneself to someone else, and what was unpleasant about being led. It could be useful to put down something on the responsibilities of being in a position of trust during that part of the session where not only the obvious leaders, but everyone was responsible for others. It may not be very productive to generalise about the nature of leadership in abstract terms at this stage but students should be encouraged to go back to their personal responses during the lesson, and try to describe them.

They may also wish to write a letter as one of the escapers, describing what it was like to make the journey across the obstacles. The less literate may wish to draw an escape map for other escapers, pointing out places where special care may need to be taken.

Follow-up Work

There is no performance element in this work. However, a silent sequence in a film could be planned, on paper, as a collection of drawings, a list of shots, or a brief story line. It could also be recorded on video, perhaps 'on location', out of doors. A group who is keen to re-enact this situation for other people to watch might like to consider the problem of conveying action which happens in darkness, to an audience who need to see, as well as hear. How effective would it be if the audience were in darkness and the actors carried torches? How much stage lighting could one use? Can actors convey a sense of being in the dark whilst remaining in normal, bright light?

This was a silent scenario. Students may like to suggest and act out other scenes of escape which perhaps are not silent. Ideas may range from sinking ships to mining disasters. The theme to be followed is that of the group being responsible for the safety of all its members.

There are many examples from fiction and real life where people have escaped through good leadership and trust. Students and teacher may be able to find some examples to share and discuss with the rest. Resource sheet 20 *Underground to Canada*, and resource sheets 21–21B, *The Smallest Pawns in the Game* are examples and either of these may be used to structure another piece of drama.

LESSON 2

Group Identity

One of the crucial factors in building up a good group identity in improvisation is the ability to listen. This may be seen as another form of trust, in that we have to trust those people to whom we tell revealing things; these things could be real facts about ourselves, or they could be part of the drama but in either case they should be treated with respect. It is also important that members of a drama group should not be afraid of physical contact and this is why holding hands, normally a threatening situation for young people, is introduced into the scene.

Preparation

RESOURCE SHEETS 22–22A
Optional:
Large handbell

After the first practical exercise, the teacher should read from resource sheet 22–22A *The Diary of Anne Frank* (see Practical Work 7) and this may require some introduction. It is certain that there will need to be some discussion about trust in other people, and the responsibility of sharing other people's secrets and the teacher may decide to discuss resource sheet 22 at the beginning rather than the end of the lesson. When practical work begins it is desirable that a quiet atmosphere is maintained and students should be encouraged to talk quietly and concentrate on their partner. If a darkened room is helpful, then that may be achieved merely by turning out the lights, without blacking out the room completely. A drama room with good facilities may benefit the students by having the lighting set at a very low level. The first practical exercise is done with eyes shut so obstacles will need to be stacked safely out of the way. A loud bell may be a useful adjunct to the improvised 'frontier' scene which follows.

Practical Work

1 IN PAIRS. (With an experienced group students may be asked to choose as a partner someone they trust, with an inexperienced group, this might cause trouble and should be left out.) All the As stand in a circle facing out, all the Bs stand opposite their partners making an inward facing circle. The teacher tells them that they are going to move round the circle in a minute with their eyes shut and that the only way they will be able to identify their partners is by feeling their hands, so they must get to know, by touch, their partner's hands. Rings, watches, etc., are allowed although it is more fun if they are removed as well. When they are ready, all the As join hands in their circle, and all the Bs join hands in theirs. They shut their eyes and are told that they should not open them again, nor should they speak a word, until they have found their partners, when they may open their eyes and go together to the side of the room. Once there they may be able to help other people by guiding them gently away from obstacles. The circles are told to move round in opposite directions. They are told to stop and release hands, then find their partners.

Naturally everyone moves about freely and in different directions; the circling was merely an initial control. The last few pairs may be guided toward each other so that they do not feel too alone.

2 The students will want to talk to each other immediately. After a while the teacher should call them together and, first, question them about how it felt to be looking for, and not finding a partner, and secondly, what it felt like when they did find their true partners. Was it a relief? Did it seem a very long time? Was there any sense of worry, or panic?

3 The teacher should then move the discussion on to the idea of reunion with someone after a long absence. The scenario is that of people who are going to be separated for many years, perhaps for ever. The As are the older by several years, (perhaps a parent or an older brother or sister). The younger one is being sent away to live in another country. The older one is holding both of the younger one's hands and relating those personal and important things that should be remembered about the old life. The teacher should quietly remind the class that they will find it useful to remember their partners' hands. They should look often at each other's hands during the telling. Students should only decide on the relationship between them before they begin, and how old the younger one is; the rest should emerge during what is said by the older one.

4 When they have finished, and at a given signal, the As should be told to go silently to one end of the room and face the wall. The Bs should go to the other end, and do likewise.

The teacher says that the scene is at a railway station, at a time when the border between two countries has been opened. B is travelling by train to pay a return visit to the country of his or her birth where A still lives. It is now twelve years since they parted. At first it may be hard for each of them to find their partners, but when they do finally recognise each other they should take each other's hands, go and sit somewhere quietly and talk, still looking down at each other's hands whenever possible. What does B remember? Does A remember too? Are things still the same? What has changed?

5 Having described the situation, the teacher then asks them to turn round and move slowly towards each other, looking out for what they remember about their partner's hands. They then play out the scenes.

6 At some appropriate time the teacher may ring the bell, jarringly and unexpectedly, and say in a loud voice that the frontier is going to close and that all those who came on the train must return. The frontier is closing and they must say goodbye. They must turn around and walk away from each other without looking back.

7 It is to be hoped that the students will appreciate some level of emotional involvement in this drama, but even without this they should be able to discuss the degree to which they felt themselves able to take the situation seriously. The teacher might begin by asking whether the concentration on hands helped or hindered the drama. Did the real situation of the first exercise help towards the imagined situation of the second? Which did they enjoy the most? Were there times when they could believe in the drama, and if so, what was it that helped to create that belief? Did they trust their partner to take them seriously?

It is at this stage that resource sheets 22–22A,

from *The Diary of Anne Frank* might be introduced, if it was not used at the beginning of the lesson. There is also some value in coming back to it following the practical work. After reading it aloud the teacher might like to set up a scene from the *Diary*.

Written Work

Some of the students might like to record the stories that unfolded during the drama in the form of a personal diary, or by making a tape either individually or as a pair. If there are some who for any reason do not wish to do so, they can still explore the theme of trusting others with personal stories by undertaking to conduct interviews, as if for a documentary programme. They will have to ask sympathetic questions, and be able to listen sensitively. These interviews or diaries and tapes might form the basis for a form of shared experience. It could be presented in the shape of a 'published' book or display of reminiscences where the students give permission for their work to be made public to the rest of the group. If it is possible to have selections typed and put together this gives status to the work.

Follow-up Work

Even if it has not been possible to record or share the stories of these reunions it should be possible for some of those who can remember the drama to tell the circumstances of their story briefly to the others. They may then be able to suggest other scenes which it would be worthwhile to add. For example, who else is involved? Did they ever meet again? What was life like in the intervening years?

It is also possible that some members of the class have family experiences which are real, and which could be made available to the others. Some of those who have had a similar experience may be prepared to come and talk to the students about it. Can the students listen positively to such direct evidence?

LESSON 3

Communication and Understanding

The ability to listen is of supreme importance in group drama, but the ability to understand and to communicate in ways other than a common language is also important in our multi-tongued culture. This session takes the ability to listen sympathetically a stage further than Lesson 2 and is seen as part of a distinct progression.

Preparation

RESOURCE SHEETS 23–24

There is little special preparation of the room for this lesson and no resource material is needed for the practical work. The teacher will naturally want to make the objectives quite clear to the class, before they begin, in order that they may be able to assess their ability to support others, and to help to promote the activity from within the drama.

Practical Work

1 IN PAIRS, students are asked to conduct a conversation in which they may only say the days of the week. It might sound like this:

A: Sunday!
B: Sunday monday wednesday...Thursday.
A: Friday? Friday, tuesday wednesday saturday, etc.

This exercise will inevitably be noisy, unless the teacher asks for it to be conducted in a whisper. After a reasonable time, the teacher should ask how many of the conversations turned out to be arguments? Differences of opinion? Persuasions? It is likely that, because they did not understand the exact meaning of the words, they picked up and exaggerated a tone of voice which became aggressive, even if whispered.

2 As an experiment the students may try the exercise again to see whether they can adopt deliberately non-belligerent attitudes; for example, one may be afraid and the other encouraging, or one sad and the other sympathetic.

3 Discuss how it is that tones of voice and body language can convey such strong images of aggression and submission, even without the sense of the words being apparent. Maybe it is possible that people in a strange land, or children who do not understand all the words can still become a part of some situation and know what is going on.

4 IN GROUPS of four try an experiment to see whether two people using the days of the week as their language can explain something to two people who can only communicate by using the months of the year. How much gesture can they use? What happens if they use a very few real words? 'Sunday monday highstreet wednesday thursday tuesday' might become utterly comprehensible by the intonation of the words as well as their meaning.

5 This is probably not an exercise that needs much discussion, but the teacher will need to pull it together before it becomes too hilarious, or too noisy. Some discussion points that may arise are the ability to understand one's partner's 'language' as well as the 'foreign' language; also whether the foreigners were shouted at as though they could not hear, or were thought of as stupid for not understanding.

6 In the same groups of four or five, let one pair be a couple of refugees, perhaps bearing some similarity to the people in Lesson 2. The others are welfare officers in their new country who have found them a place to stay in a disused airforce base. Using only months or days of the week try to show the refugees where they can sleep, cook and wash.

7 The discussion should focus on whether the refugees felt threatened by the others, and how much they managed to understand. Was it language or was it the difference in culture that made things difficult?

8 IN PAIRS. A is a police constable, B is a very young child who is the only witness to a very serious crime. After the participants have decided what the crime is, let the police constable question the child without frightening him or her. It is probably useful to suggest that it is the language and the means of communication that are important in this scene, and that B should not try to act like a baby, but to think about what a child's understanding of the terrible scene might be.

9 THE WHOLE GROUP. The teacher might set up a scene in which all those who took the part of the children are now acting as advisers to the police on methods of interviewing young children, whilst those who played the police keep the same roles. Using the experience of the interviews in the previous scenes the teacher can chair an in-role discussion about the ways in which vital evidence can be obtained in a non-threatening way. The subject of child abuse may be introduced by the class, in or out of role; it is up to the teacher whether to tackle this in the context of police and courtroom procedure or whether to take it on to a more serious and personal level.

Written Work

If possible the students should try to record the interviews with the children fairly quickly. In role they should be able to put down how the child remembered being questioned or how the police constable tried to make a child understand. It is also important that they try to pin-point the degree of sensitivity that they were able to see in each other and in themselves. If the ability to listen to each other is important then students should be encouraged to record the effects of that focus, both on the drama, and on the strength of the group.

Follow-up Work

Some of the written interviews may offer material for further scenes. It may be possible to build up the whole story of one of those incidents by adding other characters. An interesting way of continuing the idea of listening would be to have the child repeat the story at various stages of his or her lifetime. How would people tell the story in the first year of secondary school? Would they ever tell it? Make a soliloquy of it, as if by an old person, speaking thoughts aloud.

Students might like to read and discuss the scene in resource sheet 23, *Kes*, and relate it to the stories they have previously written as interviews. Why could Billy explain something about his feelings to Mr Farthing, but not to Mr Gryce? Alternatively, resource sheet 24 gives examples of newspaper reports concerning children. Students could use these as a basis for interview scenes.

LESSON 4

The Group under Pressure

The work in this lesson leads on from some of the ideas about group identity already introduced. It is intended to deepen familiarity with ways of working collaboratively and, at the same time, gives practice in putting together a complete play. There is no physical warm-up to this lesson, but teachers may wish to introduce one if the class needs it.

Preparation

> RESOURCE SHEETS 25–26
> Paper and pencils
> Clipboards or desks
> Chairs

Students will need copies of both resource sheets. The 'foreign language' resource sheet 25 is used as an introduction, the 'English language' form, resource sheet 26 is for the longer section of the drama. Most of the drama is fairly static and only chairs, and perhaps desks or clipboards to write on are necessary. Any other aids to the drama are entirely at the teacher's discretion. The theme will need to be introduced to the students through discussion of the probable reasons for people to leave their homeland, with special reference to the political implications of the escape drama they have already done.

Practical Work

1 IN GROUPS of three or four, one is appointed as 'the official' the others are refugees. The groups are spread about three sides of the room; the other side is for the officials and the teacher. The teacher sets up the situation of a very bewildered group of refugees who are seeking asylum in a foreign country. They will need a few moments to discuss their relationship and background, based on their previous work.

The teacher then assumes the role of chief official and calls over the other officials to collect forms and writing implements and explains, in a very low voice, that officials cannot speak English but must get these forms filled up by immigrants immediately. The officials are to be indifferent to immigrants' problems but may look at the forms first so as to familiarise themselves with the sound of the language. Officials are given numbers so that they can be called to the teacher for whispered consultation at any time, otherwise only refugees can speak to each other in their own language. (In a multilingual class this may not be English.)

The filling up of the forms should cause a highly pressured situation to develop and officials may collect and redistribute forms at the will of the teacher or 'correct' the wording at their own desire.

The end may be arranged in two ways. Either the officials are called together and given English forms to distribute, in which case the drama continues uninterrupted, or the teacher calls a halt to discuss the first part and allows the groups to talk about their collective reasons for wanting to come in to a safe country. The confusion over language and the strangeness of the situation should, however, remain as an important part of the drama.

2 The English language forms are completed, with the help of the officials, who can now interpret if necessary. When they have been checked with the chief official; instructions can be given to question the refugees, kindly but firmly, to ascertain their suitability to come into the country. They must be capable of supporting themselves and there must not be too many sick, old or very young people, who would be a drain on the resources of the host country. They are also to treat as suspicious any aggressive or resentful behaviour and refer such behaviour to the chief official, who may have to issue warnings about suitability for adoption into the country.

3 It is to be hoped that the drama will continue uninterrupted until such time as the teacher calls the officials together with their recommendations. They will then inform their groups of their destiny: 'in', or 'out'.

4 There will need to be a final discussion of this drama; it is important to gather any first-hand experiences of coming into foreign territory, even if these only involve coming to school for the first time or moving from one part of the country to another. The difficulties of communicating in English as a 'foreign' language could also form part of the discussion.

Written Work

Letters from a foreign country to friends at home are one form of creative writing which could follow on from this lesson. Alternatively, students could be asked to write about the attitude towards immigrant people adopted by the country presented in their drama. Taped interviews with refugees, a TV documentary, interviews with real refugees or immigrants are further ideas. From the drama viewpoint, students may wish to say something about their place in this group and whether they found it constructive.

Follow-up Work

There are a number of scenes which may be built up around this topic as the refugees settle into their new country or find themselves having to stay in camps.

LESSON 5

The Individual within the Group

In this lesson the same process is applied to a very different set of circumstances. It is seen as providing an opportunity for a change of role and a more advanced level of character-building within the group. Those students who played guards in the previous lesson should have an opportunity of taking a waif's role in this lesson.

Preparation

```
RESOURCE SHEETS 27–29
Chairs
Optional:
Large cardboard boxes
Cloth and blankets
Tables
```

After photocopying the two pages of resource sheets 28–28A, they should be cut up into separate pictures. The teacher will take the part of Dr Barnardo, but the name is not important and the students may simply refer to the role as 'that kind lady' or some such definition. There should be chairs in the room and a clutter of tables, odd bits of scenery, cardboard boxes, cloths and bits of blanket may be an asset.

Practical Work

Some groups may need to talk about the position of young people who are rendered homeless or who choose to leave home and take to the streets. Others may want to go into the drama straight away.

1 After consulting the drawings and caption on resource sheet 27, the teacher should adopt Barnardo's role and make a short speech pleading the case for increased public concern over the plight of homeless children. Some in role discussion should follow about responsibility for destitute young people. Out of this there should be sufficient material to move smoothly to the next stage. If the subject does not arouse much in the way of opposing attitudes then the drama should stop, whilst the teacher introduces the idea for the next scene.

2 The students should be asked to recreate the scene in picture (a) of resource sheet 27. The teacher will be Barnardo and some students should be chosen to represent the adults who came with him. (These are not seen in the picture.) After they have looked at the group of waifs on the roof the 'adults' should first hold a low-voiced conference and then try to coax the children to talk, with the bribe of hot tea from a nearby stall. The motive for the chat is to find out how these children are placed and whether they will come to a meeting the next day, in an empty warehouse.

3 At this stage two things happen together:

(a) The teacher spreads out the pictures cut from photocopies of resource sheets 28 and 28A, and asks the students to pick one that most nearly accords with the character they have begun to make for themselves. If there are some characters who, it is felt, would never have shown their faces at the meeting then the students concerned should be encouraged to change to a more responsive personality. They should be told that they will have to keep to those characters for a while and invent a likely background which would have driven them to such a poor living on the roof. Having chosen their roles, and asked any important questions, they should sit apart and think through their situations. Some may have chosen to work with a partner, and they may talk softly together; otherwise the preparation will be in silence.

(b) Meanwhile the 'adults' will be shown what they must do. They are to find out as much as they can about the youngsters, with the idea of taking as many as possible into the first Children's Home. They will need to have a time limit and they will need to be gentle, but firm. Only those children who might benefit from some kind of training will be taken. They may set up an interview space.

4 Dr Barnardo calls the children together and tells them about his plans for a children's home. He sends them in small groups to give their names to the interviewers. Interviews go on as long as there are children to come forward, but any who are restless or causing problems may be referred to the Doctor. Finally, the interviewers are called together, in the hearing of the children, to discuss the desirability of admitting some or excluding some. The Doctor will be able to quash any likelihood of partiality or silliness at this stage. The children are told the result of the interviews. There may very well be some in-role discussion about the lack of humility in some, or the splitting up of family groups, or the reasons why some did not get in. At this point the lesson ends. Any spare time may be given over to discussion of the lesson.

Written Work

Many of Dr Barnardo's children would have been unable to read or write; however, by accepting that their stories have been dictated to someone else, students who played children could write a biography to go with a copy of their child's picture, either for their folders, or for the wall of the drama room. Interviewers may write up their official notes on each character. No other written work is suggested because it is important at this stage that the students concentrate on a review of their work using the Unit 3 student assessment form.

Follow-up Work

Dr Barnardo was accused of having forged the photographs of children in order to arouse sympathy and to get more money for his work. It might be interesting to call children as witnesses in the trial of Dr Barnardo. It may also be interesting to look at the whole picture of Victorian child care, and make a documentary, which links it with the present day. Resource sheet 29, on the young homeless today may be used in this context.

The Diary of Anne Frank

Sunday, 5th July, 1942

Dear Kitty,

When we walked across our little square together a few days ago, Daddy began to talk of us going into hiding. I asked him why on earth he was beginning to talk of that already. "Yes, Anne," he said, "you know that we have been taking food, clothes, furniture to other people for more than a year now. We don't want our belongings to be seized by the Germans, and we certainly don't want to fall into their clutches ourselves. So we shall disappear of our own accord and not wait until they come and fetch us."

"But Daddy, when would it be?" He spoke so seriously that I grew very anxious.

"Don't you worry about it, we shall arrange everything. Make the most of your carefree young life while you can." That was all. Oh, may the fulfilment of these sombre words remain far distant yet!

Yours, Anne

Wednesday, 8th July, 1942

Dear Kitty,

Years seemed to have passed between Sunday and now. So much has happened, it is just as if the whole world had turned upside down. But I am still alive, Kitty, and that is the main thing, Daddy says.

Yes, I'm still alive, indeed, but don't ask where or how. You wouldn't understand a word, so I will begin by telling you what happened on Sunday afternoon.

At three o'clock (Harry had just gone, but was coming back later) someone rang the front door bell. I was lying lazily reading a book on the veranda in the sunshine, so didn't hear it. A bit later, Margot appeared at the kitchen door looking very excited. "The S.S. have sent a call-up notice for Daddy," she whispered. "Mummy has gone to see Mr. Van Daan already." (Van Daan is a friend who works with Daddy in the business.) It was a great shock to me, a call-up; everyone knows what that means. I picture concentration camps and lonely cells – should we allow him to be doomed to this? "Of course he won't go," declared Margot, while we waited together. "Mummy has gone to the Van Daans to discuss whether we should move into our hiding-place tomorrow. The Van Daans are going with us, so we shall be seven in all." Silence. We couldn't talk any more, thinking about Daddy, who, little knowing what was going on, was visiting some old people in the Joodse Invalide; waiting for Mummy, the heat and suspense, all made us very overawed and silent.

Suddenly the bell rang again. "That is Harry," I said. "Don't open the door." Margot held me back, but it was not necessary as we heard Mummy and Mr. Van Daan downstairs, talking to Harry, then they came in and closed the door behind them. Each time the bell went, Margot or I had to creep softly down to see if it was Daddy, not opening the door to anyone else.

Margot and I were sent out of the room. Van Daan wanted to talk to Mummy alone. When we were alone together in our bedroom, Margot told me that the call-up was not for Daddy, but for her. I was more frightened than ever and began to cry. Margot is sixteen; would they really take girls of that age away alone? But thank goodness she won't go. Mummy said so herself; that must be what Daddy meant when he talked about us going into hiding.

Into hiding – where would we go, in a town or the country, in a house or a cottage, when, how, where. . .?

These were questions I was not allowed to ask, but I couldn't get them out of my mind. Margot and I began to pack some of our most vital belongings into a school satchel. The first thing I put in was this diary, then hair-curlers, handkerchiefs, school books, a comb, old letters; I put in the craziest things with the idea that we were going into hiding. But I'm not sorry, memories mean more to me than dresses.

At five o'clock Daddy finally arrived, and we rang up Mr. Koophuis to ask if he could come round in the evening. Van Daan went and fetched Miep. Miep has been in the business with Daddy since 1933 and has become a close friend, likewise her brand-new husband, Henk. Miep came and took some shoes, dresses, coats, underwear, and stockings away in her bag, promising to return in the evening. Then silence fell on the house; not one of us felt like eating anything, it was still hot and everything was very strange. We let our large upstairs room to a certain Mr. Goudsmit, a divorced man in the thirties, who appeared to have nothing to do on this particular evening; we simply could not get rid of him without being rude; he hung about until ten o'clock. At eleven o'clock Miep and Henk Van Santen arrived. Once again, shoes, stockings, books, and underclothes disappeared into Miep's bag and Henk's deep pockets, and at eleven-thirty they too disappeared. I was dog-tired, and although I knew that it would be my last night in my own bed I fell asleep immediately and didn't wake up until Mummy called me at 5.30 the next morning. Luckily it was not so hot as Sunday; warm rain fell steadily all day. We put on heaps of clothes as if we were going to the North Pole, the sole reason being to take clothes with us. No Jew in our situation would have dreamt of going out with a suitcase full of clothing. I had on two vests, three pairs of knickers, a dress, on top of that a skirt, jacket, summer coat, two pairs of stockings, lace-up shoes, woolly cap, scarf and still more; I was nearly stifled before we started, but no one inquired about that.

Margot filled her satchel with school books, fetched her bicycle and rode off behind Miep into the unknown, as far as I was concerned. You see I still didn't know where our secret hiding-place was to be. At seven thirty the door closed behind us. Moortie, my little cat, was the only creature to whom I said farewell. She would have a good home with the neighbours. This was all written in a letter addressed to Mr. Goudsmit.

There was one pound of meat in the kitchen for the cat, breakfast things lying on the table, stripped beds, all giving the impression that we had left helter-skelter. But we didn't care about impressions, we only wanted to get away, only escape and arrive safely, nothing else. Continued tomorrow.

Yours, Anne

Thursday, 9th July, 1942

Dear Kitty,

So we walked in the pouring rain, Daddy, Mummy, and I, each with a school satchel and shopping bag filled to the brim with all kinds of things thrown together anyhow.

We got sympathetic looks from people on their way to work. You could see by their faces how sorry they were they couldn't offer us a lift; the gaudy yellow star spoke for itself.

Only when we were on the road did Mummy and Daddy begin to tell me bits and pieces about the plan. For months as many of our goods and chattels and necessities of life as possible had been sent away and things were sufficiently ready for us to have gone into hiding of our own accord on 16th July. The plan had had to be speeded up ten days because of the call-up, so our quarters would not be so well organised, but we had to make the best of it. The hiding-place itself would be in the building where Daddy has his office.

Yours, Anne

Friday, 10th July, 1942

Dear Kitty,

I expect I have thoroughly bored you with my long-winded descriptions of our dwelling. But still I think you should know where we've landed.

But to continue my story — you see, I've not finished yet — when we arrived at the Prinsengracht, Miep took us quickly upstairs and into the "Secret Annexe." She closed the door behind us and we were alone. Margot was already waiting for us, having come much faster on her bicycle. Our living-room and all the other rooms were chock full of rubbish, indescribably so. All the cardboard boxes which had been sent to the office in the previous months lay piled on the floor and the beds. The little room was filled to the ceiling with bedclothes. We had to start clearing up immediately, if we wished to sleep in decent beds that night. Mummy and Margot were not fit to move a muscle; they lay on the unmade beds, tired, miserable, and lots more besides. But the two "clearers-up" of the family – Daddy and myself – wanted to start at once.

The whole day long we unpacked boxes, filled cupboards, hammered and tidied, until deadbeat. We sank into clean beds that night. We hadn't had a bit of anything warm the whole day, but we didn't care; Mummy and Margot were too tired and keyed up to eat, and Daddy and I were too busy.

On Tuesday morning we went on where we left off the day before. Elli and Miep collected our rations for us, Daddy improved the poor black-out, we scrubbed the kitchen floor, and were on the go the whole day long again.

I hardly had time to think about the great change in my life until Wednesday. Then I had a chance, for the first time since our arrival, to tell you all about it, and at the same time to realise myself what had actually happened to me and what was still going to happen.

Yours, Anne

(abridged) ANNE FRANK

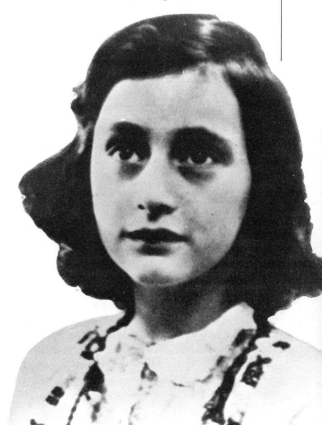

Kes

'All right, lad, calm down. It's finished with now.'
He waited for him to calm down, then shook his head slowly.
'I don't know, you always seem to cop it, don't you, Casper?'
Billy stood with his head bowed, sniffing quietly to himself.
'I wonder why? Why do you think it is?'
'What, Sir?'
'That you're always in trouble?'
''Cos everybody picks on me, that's why.'
He looked up with such intensity that his eyes and the tears webbed in the lower lashes seemed to fuse and shine like lumps of crystal. Mr Farthing looked away to hide a smile.
'Yes I know they do, but why?'
'I don't know, they just do, that's all.'
'Perhaps it's because you're a bad lad.'
'P'raps I am, sometimes. But I'm not that bad, I'm no worse than stacks o' kids, but they just seem to get away with it.'
'You think you're just unlucky, then?'
'I don't know, Sir. I seem to get into bother for nowt. You know, for daft things, like this morning in t'hall. I wasn't doin' owt, I just dozed off that's all. I wa' dog tired, I'd been up since six, then I'd had to run round wi' t'papers, then run home to have a look at t'hawk, then run to school. We', I mean, you'd be tired wouldn't you, Sir?'
Mr Farthing chuckled.
'I'd be exhausted.'
'That's nowt to get t'stick for, is it Sir, being tired? You can't tell Gryce...Mr Gryce though, he'd kill you! Do you know, Sir, there wa' a kid this morning stood outside his room wi' us, he'd only brought a message from another teacher, and Mr Gryce gave him t'stick!'
Mr Farthing's face broadened into a grin, and his mouth broke open, laughing. Billy watched these changes in expression seriously.
'It's all right for you, Sir. What about that kid though, he was as sick as a dog after.'
Mr Farthing immediately became serious again.
'You're right, lad, it's not funny. It was just the way you told it, that's all.'
'An' this morning in English, when I wasn't listening. It wasn't that I wasn't bothered, it wa' my hands, they were killin' me! You can't concentrate when your hands are stingin' like mad!'
'No, I don't suppose you can.'
'I still got into trouble for it though, didn't I?'
'You made up for it though, didn't you?'
'I know, but it's allus like that though.'
'What is?'
'Teachers. They never think it might be their fault an' all.'
'No, I don't think many do, lad.'

BARRY HINES

RESOURCE SHEET 24

Kidnap girl freed in dawn raid

A SPANISH anti-terrorist officer shot a French gangster using five-year-old kidnap victim Melodie Nakachian, the daughter of a Lebanese millionaire, as a shield and snatched her unharmed from his grip in a pre-dawn raid in the shadow of the Rock of Gibraltar yesterday.

Police located the French kidnappers in a small holiday villa near the frontier town of San Roque after one of the gang out jogging in a nearby resort lost his wallet, containing a blue print for the £2.27 million ransom demand, and it was found by a woman and handed in to the police.

Melodie's first words when she was reunited with her mother, Korean opera star Kimera, at the family's villa near Marbella were: "Don't cry Mummy, I'm all right."

Since she had been kidnapped 12 days ago while on her way to school, Melodie had been fed only on cake and had lost 3lb in weight.

'Fantastic police'

But her father said his daughter had not been ill-treated and that the kidnappers had bought her a new dress.

Mr Nakachian said: "She has stood up to the ordeal rather better than the rest of the family. We haven't slept for days but the police have been fantastic."

He also said the kidnappers had cut off locks of Melodie's hair, which they had sent to him along with two photographs and cassette tapes of Melodie pleading for the ransom to be paid.

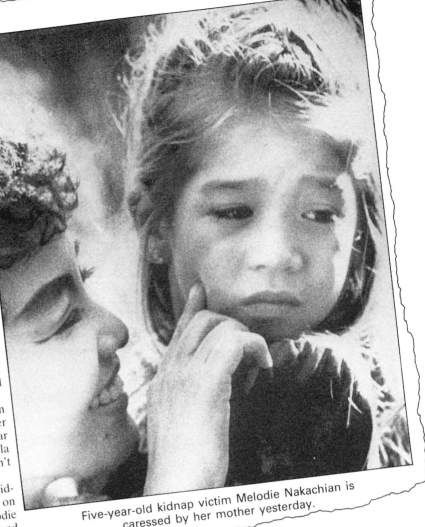

Five-year-old kidnap victim Melodie Nakachian is caressed by her mother yesterday.

Triple-murder hunt after house fire

Police have begun a murder inquiry after a nurse and two of her sons were found in their burning home in Redhill, Surrey. Detectives believe six-year-old Robert Smith and his brother, Christopher, aged four, were killed by an intruder who then started a fire.

Police are not sure whether Columbian-born Mrs Esneda Smith, who was separated from her husband, was killed by intruder or died from fumes.

They are waiting to talk to the only survivor, seven-year-old Stephen Smith, who is in Queen Victoria Hospital, East Grinstead.

RESOURCE SHEET 25

Foreign Immigration form

2
ZADOST O .... CIZUM

Prijmeni		Jmeno		Poznavaci znacka	Statni prislusmost	Mezinarodni zn. Muzzena
Adresa zadatele – stat	Mesto		Ulice			
Den, mesic a rok narozeni	Misto narozeni – stat		Mesto	Tovarni znacka vazidla	Barva vazidla	
Povolani	Nazev podniku			Mesto		
Adresy pobytu – mesto	Ulice		Prijmeni osoby nebo nazev hotelu			
Ucel cesty do CS	Doba pobytu v CS	Spolucestujici detl do 15 let				
Razitko PK – ODJEZD			Razitko PK – PRIJEZD			
Podpls						

RESOURCE SHEET 26

English Immigration Form

DEPARTMENT OF IMMIGRATION

1 Name and title

2 Age

3 Country of Origin

4 Names and ages of any dependent relatives

5 Reasons for wishing to enter this country

6 Trade or skills

RESOURCE SHEET 27

Dr Barnardo had been taken by a destitute boy to a 'lay' in a mouldering wharf where other homeless children slept, unprotected, on an iron roof. Some days later, when the speaker at a missionary conference failed to arrive, Barnardo was asked to deputise. As a result of his passionate plea for these waifs Lord Shaftesbury invited him to supper, on condition that he would show some sceptical guests the homeless children he had described. Barnardo accepted the challenge and, after much fruitless searching, in the early hours of the morning they found seventy-two shivering children, lying under a tarpaulin in a street near Billingsgate.

RESOURCE SHEET 28

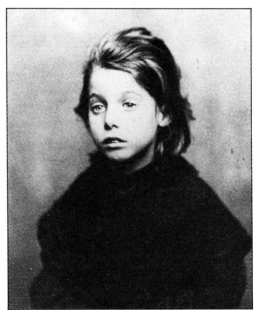
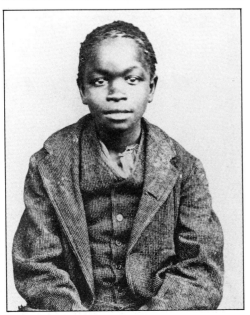

RESOURCE SHEET 28A

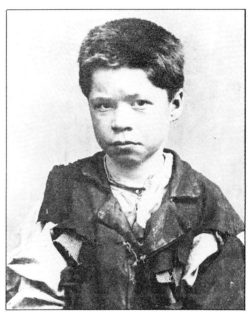

RESOURCE SHEET 29

Youth shelters in concrete boot

FOR TWO MONTHS Mark has lived in a giant concrete boot in a children's adventure playground. Inside, it is a stinking tunnel, like a fox's earth, carpeted with snow, broken glass, Coke cans and rags. One of the rags is Mark's blanket, which has frozen solid since somebody urinated on it.

At the Centrepoint night hostel in Shaftesbury Avenue they have taken in 2000 children in the past year, and turned another 2000 away. The director, Nick Hardwick, tells us that 16 years ago the maximum age was 25; then it was lowered to 21 and now it is 19, such is the pressure of numbers.

"Anyone who looks like they can survive on the street we have to turn away, and we can't keep anyone more than a couple of nights."

Every night a volunteer sleeps in the spartan dormitory with the 30 or so children, partly to keep order but more often to comfort those who cry in the night.

STUDENT ASSESSMENT (UNIT 3)

The emphasis in this unit was on group work. Looking back on the tasks you were given you will find that you were part of a number of different groups both in the drama and in the class.

1 How does the class work together as a whole group? If there are any difficulties can you suggest ways in which these might be overcome?

2 In working with others in a group what sort of contributions do you make? Do you find it easy to make suggestions? Can you take other people's suggestions?

3 In what way is drama about large groups of people interesting, or exciting?

4 How far were you able to believe in the situations that you acted out? What helped to build your belief?

5 What was the most useful piece of written, or follow-up work that you did in this unit? What do you think you learned from the work as a whole?

Unit 4 Building a Character

This is the title of a well-known book on acting by Konstantin Stanislavsky. (*Building a Character* by Konstantin Stanislavsky, translated by Elizabeth Reynolds-Hapgood, Reinhardt and Evans, 1950.) Although written for actors as part of their professional training, it nevertheless applies to a great deal of drama work with young people. There comes a moment in which the group has to face up to their ability to create belief in a topic or characters and then to make sure that others can believe them as well.

This ability is not one which can be developed just before a performance. Its acquisition is an integral part of the work; without that necessary suspension of disbelief very little depth can be achieved in drama, whatever the teacher's ultimate objectives may be.

The object of this unit is to build background and context for a set of differing characters and situations. The greater burden of study will, of necessity, be on the individual student. It will be the teacher's responsibility to motivate the individual in a productive fashion in order that private study can be perceived to be worthwhile.

LESSON 1

Establishing a Base

Every character should have a background and environment and Stanislavsky encouraged his students to build that background for themselves. In this case it is a single room.

Preparation

> RESOURCE SHEETS 30–31
> Paper and pencils
> Blackboard or large sheet of paper for teacher

No resource materials are required for the practical work in this lesson. A large space will be needed if there are many students in the group. The structure of the whole unit should be discussed at the beginning of the session so that any questions can be dealt with at once, and students prepared for the fact that they will be expected to work on their own for some of the time.

Practical Work

1 The teacher should introduce the lesson by discussing the implications of the word 'apartment'; not just the practical layout of such a place, but the sense of separate lives, led 'apart'. Students are told that a rather run-down, large building has been converted into single-room apartments by the local authority. They are each allocated a number for their apartment and given a sheet of paper on which to write the name of the person who lives in it. The teacher should make a note of names and numbers and determine who lives on the top floor, the basement and so on. This information having been put onto a plan on a large sheet of paper or a blackboard and thus made public, the students then take themselves off and 'move in' to their allocated space by unpacking their things and setting their new home to rights. They should be told to establish the exact position of washbasin, windows, etc., as they put things away. After a time the teacher should ask them to sit down in their space. In turn each character should then put their name outside the 'door' of their room and in a couple of sentences describe what that person feels about moving in there. It may be necessary at this stage to ask them not to fuss about the fact that boundaries may cross; if someone walks through their wall, they must just ignore it.

2 The characters may now meet each other. At first it will be the next-door neighbour who comes for help to move a bed, to borrow a cup of sugar, to be shown around the apartment or exchange visits. The teacher should remind them that the papers with names on represent the door of each apartment. These visits may well go beyond a simple exchange, but there may also be those who make no contact at all. It is usually wise not to encourage too many recluses or refugees from justice at this stage.

3 The teacher should send them back to their chairs and ask them to describe their neighbours, in role. Their reactions may be coloured by their own personalities, and they may have very strong reasons for liking or disliking each other.

Students should be encouraged to listen carefully to their own and everyone else's role description. They should be able to take the information given as useful material for the next part of the lesson. If necessary the teacher should interview characters a little in order to round out the information being offered.

4 After a while the teacher should discuss with the whole group which stories or personalities suggest the basis of a play. It could have a very simple beginning such as a new landlady taking over, or it could be that a suspicious situation seems to be developing round one of the characters. After discussing how some of the characters see themselves responding to this situation, plan a beginning to the drama, choose a time of day and begin. The teacher should watch to see how the play develops and be ready to intervene as a supernumerary character if one is needed. As soon as the play seems to have got well under way, the teacher may interrupt in order to discuss with the students, out of character, what exactly the plot is revealing, how it is shaping up, what lines of development are becoming apparent and whether each character has enough room to grow. If some students are having difficulty fitting into the situation the others may have to find a way of bringing them into the drama. This kind of constructive planning is a good exercise in group co-operation.

5 The teacher should give the students a time limit within which they should try to bring the situation to a satisfactory ending. If there seems to be no possibility of an ending, the teacher may intervene as a character in the play and call a public meeting or ask everyone to present themselves at the police station the next day, or some such device that seems appropriate to the situation.

6 The session should be rounded off by the teacher, who summarises the story for the group. This may be difficult if there is a great deal of overlap or confusion of scenes all happening at once. The problems of focus in a large group may be discussed, but the main objective of the play is nevertheless to establish character and the teacher should try to bring this out in the summary of the lesson.

Written Work

Students should be given copies of resource sheet 30, *Feiffer monologues*. This may be used as a reference point for creating monologues for the characters they have already built up. These may be 'performed' if the students wish or they may be collected together as a picture of a community. Dylan Thomas's opening to *Under Milk Wood*, resource sheet 31, may be read as an example of a way of setting up scene and character to suggest a whole community.

Follow-up Work

If there is enough meat in the characters that have emerged from all the work on the 'apartment' stories, then it should be possible to look at ways of focusing on one small unit and then shifting to another within the same play. A structure derived from the British model of television soap opera could be used to practise movement from one short scene to another within the same basic environment or scenario. Some students may be motivated to write such a basic outline, either by themselves or as part of a team. This could then be used as part of an attempt to create a complete play. Alternatively they may prefer to carry on with improvised drama in an attempt to strengthen the characters by working on them in greater detail and in relationship to other characters.

LESSON 2

One in a Crowd

Regimented crowds offer little interest for the actor, unless they are made up of individual characters. It is up to the actor to provide a rationale for the unidentified 'face in the crowd'.

Preparation

> RESOURCE SHEETS 32–32A
> Pencils
> Optional:
> Rostra
> Smoke machine or talcum powder
> Source of coloured light

After the initial exercise, students will need individual copies of resource sheets 32–32A, *The Fall of Troy*. Pencils are needed to mark up the script. This scene was written for women, but in the original Greek play the parts were probably played by men. In a class of boys there should be no difficulty in playing this scene seriously, dealing as it does with the effects of war on the civilian population. It may be compared with the somewhat humourous depiction of the women in the scene from *Under Milk Wood*. In any class, discussion about the attitudes of the women to male aggression might prove a useful way of deepening understanding. The best avenue of approach to a sensitive area, such as this, is probably to plunge straight in and pick up any questions as they arise. What is important is to establish the method of building a background to a character who simply appears under a general description, in this case 'Women'. The purpose of the first exercise is to establish a way of picking up clues to the sources of people's attitudes which in turn helps to show how their behaviour and opinions might potentially develop.

Practical Work

1] The students should be asked to arrange chairs for an evening meeting. The teacher should tell them that the meeting will be a parents' meeting about closing the school. They are to decide two things: what sort of parent they are going to represent, and what has happened during the day to put them in a certain mood. They should decide this privately and keep it to themselves. They should then be told that during the scene they may explain what has happened to put them in this mood, or they may simply express that mood in the way they behave as a 'parent'.

2] After a few moments the teacher should announce the beginning of the meeting and ask parents to take their places. It is possible that some will choose to arrive late, but the teacher should announce that the speaker has been delayed, so would everyone please talk amongst themselves until the speaker does arrive. The timing of the scene may vary; the teacher should let it run on as long as it seems productive.

3] The teacher should apologise again for the speaker: 'In case the representative of the Education Committee doesn't manage to make it in time, perhaps those who have gone to so much trouble to come would make themselves known and say a few words about how they feel about the school being closed.' The teacher should chair the meeting and cut through any over-long dissertations; note should also be taken of the way students express mood in body language and speech usage for later discussion. It may also be necessary to cut through any out-of-character laughter, by calling on another speaker, or questioning a character or calling the meeting to order. Part of any teacher's technique in building belief in a situation is to take their own roles, and those of others, with great seriousness. After everyone has spoken, thank them and end the scene.

4] After some discussion about what mood each actor was portraying and how this information was conveyed, the teacher should read through the scene on resource sheets 32–32A, either by reading it aloud while the group follows, or by 'reading round', each student taking a separate sentence or theatrical 'line'. The part of Hecuba should be taken by a competent reader. If preferred, the students may read it through silently. At the end of the reading, the teacher should try to extract some information about the underlying mood of each line. This should be put up on a board, or on a large sheet of paper. Words like – 'angry', 'hurt', 'aggressive', 'optimistic' and 'resigned' may occur to the group from a first reading. The teacher should number these words on the board and the students should be encouraged to come to an agreement about which lines in the text express which mood (or combination of moods). They should then number the lines according to mood.

5] The next stage is to allocate moods. This may be done either by the teacher giving each student or pair of students a number, or by the students themselves identifying the characteristic mood that they portrayed in the first exercise. In either case they should now be able to read certain lines in the scene according to a chosen or given mood. They should then be able to read through the scene again to sort out exactly who is saying what. Where more than one student shares a characteristic they can decide whether to speak together or to split up the lines.

6 If there is time the students may be able to give themselves the same kind of motive for mood as they did in the first exercise, only this time it is taken from what has happened in the drama and what their characters have seen during the previous day and night's fighting. They should also be able to decide age, status and family for each woman from the information that is conveyed in the lines.

Written Work

Character biographies may be constructed from very little information other than that which is contained in the text. If the students wish to read more about the Trojan war, then such information can be found in the plays of Aeschylus and Sophocles published by Penguin Classics, and from more recent archaeological or historical sources.

Students may also be encouraged to make a sound tape of the scene where they were over-run by the enemy or a taped or written description of what they saw and felt when dawn broke on the morning after the city was destroyed. A more practical piece of writing may chart the process by which mood and situation were built up and whether this helped in approaching the text.

Follow-up Work

The scene may be rehearsed and staged. Rostra could effectively be used to suggest the ruins. A low level of light may help to give atmosphere. If the scene is to be performed before an audience then either a smoke machine may be borrowed, or hired, or a way of making and using dry ice may be sought from the chemistry teacher. Failing this, a small quantity of talcum powder puffed in front of a red lantern fixed to the floor behind a pile of rostra may be enough to suggest smoke.

LESSON 3

Physical Characteristics

Characterisation on stage requires a certain selection process. Just as at the beginning of the course students were asked to select action so as to avoid confusion and to give focus to their work, so, when working on characterisation, students need to be selective about what aspects to show and what to leave out.

Preparation

> RESOURCE SHEETS 33–34
> Supply of plastic cups

There is little preparation for this lesson other than the provision of sufficient plastic cups for each student to have one and some extra in case of accidents. A copy of resource sheet 33 is required for each student.

Practical Work

1 The teacher should introduce the subject of physical characteristics and then say that the students will begin by looking at some very extreme examples of behaviour, as a warm-up before some more serious work. The teacher explains that there is going to be a garden party to which only animals are invited. These are very important animals, chosen to represent their species. However, because of previous bad behaviour, monkeys and apes have been excluded. Without discussing it with anyone, the students should choose an animal to represent. They should be particularly aware that their animal may have to have a method of dealing with the difficulty of drinking politely out of a plastic cup. Animals should be able to speak to each other in human language if necessary. The teacher puts the plastic cups out on a table (or two if it is a large group), and announces that the party has begun.

 The teacher will be able to see whether this exercise is being taken seriously or not. It is not vital that students remain straight-faced at all times but it does affect what comes next. At some convenient point the teacher should bring the exercise to an end and the group should talk it through, concentrating on the animals' social problems of combining drinking and polite behaviour. The teacher should then set up the next exercise which consists of the same situation, only this time the guests are people who have animal characteristics. They may have a laugh like a donkey or

77

eat like a pig, they may be as scared as a mouse, or bark like a 'scotty' dog. Students should be asked to take this stage as seriously as possible and to try to recognise each other's animal characteristics by moving about and meeting other people, whilst maintaining their own character. The teacher puts the cups out again and the scene begins.

3 When the scene ends, the questioning should now be about recognition. What animal characteristics could be identified? Were there restraints, caused by the high status of the garden party? How difficult was it to recognise other peoples' work whilst keeping one's own character convincing? The next stage is to push the animal trait to a level where it becomes a nervous habit. Something the owner wants to hide. It may be that some students will need help from the teacher or other students in deciding whether they should change what they were doing and find some other nervous habit for their character. The situation remains the same. They play out the scene.

4 IN GROUPS of three or four. The teacher should now propose a topic for a television interview, or the students could submit one for the teacher's approval.

Each group then sets up a television interview in which a roving reporter is asking people absolutely serious questions on the chosen topic. The objective for this part of the lesson is to make the nervous animal habit so much part of the character that it informs rather than becomes a caricature. This is a very sophisticated exercise and may produce a great deal of hilarity, or over-acting, on the part of some students. The session may go in two directions at this point: either, the teacher may work with any group having difficulty in producing realistic characters, or, if this is a general problem, they may allow everyone to continue with the scenes as comedy. In both cases the discussion afterwards should focus on the use of individual, physical traits to give life to a character. Some students may wish to show their work at this stage. It is important to examine the nature of exaggeration, the way in which comedians take physical eccentricities as a basis for outsize characters, and the reasons why we laugh at them. It is also important that students do not fall into a habit of easy caricature as a cover for insecurity, and that the group trusts itself enough to produce work of reasonable depth. Such things may well be talked out at this time.

5 In the same, or different, groups students should now look at the Chekhov characters' speeches on resource sheet 33. Individual groups should then choose one character's speech and discuss a way of presenting the 'essence' of this character to the other groups. For example one person may represent the character physically whilst the lines are read by the other actors in the group, or there may be a whole group of Charlottas, each one agreeing with, and adding to the thoughts of the others. These character studies should be presented to the rest of the class.

Written Work

Students should be able to record their own feelings about the differences between laughing at human frailty and sympathising with it. They may need to answer a specific question such as why Chekhov describes his plays as comedies, given only the evidence from the extracts. They may wish to write their own version of a 'twenty-two misfortunes' character, either in-role as a monologue, or as a description.

Follow-up Work

Chekhov wrote some one act plays which could form the basis for further work on the presentation of character, in particular 'The Bear', or 'The Proposal', both of which may be found in the *Oxford Chekhov. Volume 1: The Short Plays*, translated by Ronald Hingley, Oxford University Press, 1968. Resource sheet 34 gives some information on the importance of Stanislavsky's work in this area. Without using text students may like to look at costume and accessories as an adjunct to presenting a character. The school may have a wardrobe or they may be able to find and borrow significant costume accessories. A collection of portrait pictures from news magazines or other sources may be one way of collecting characters to form a basis for the creation of monologues or short scenes that could be presented to other people.

LESSON 4

Character Motivation

Teachers should introduce this session by talking about the word 'motivation'. Characters are often 'motivated' to do things by a particular desire or need, and it may be necessary for actors to find that need for themselves. They should be encouraged to ask 'what is my motivation for doing this?'

The other important factor to take into account

in working on character is the sub-text. A butcher may be cutting up meat just as he does every working day, but when he is serving his secret lady-love or his hated oppressor he may well cut up the meat in a totally different frame of mind, which may affect his actions.

Preparation

> RESOURCE SHEETS 35–36
> Props, for instance:
> Telephone, playing cards, paper, buttons, newspaper, cutlery.
> Tables and chairs

Each student will need a copy of resource sheet 35, *The Boy with a Cart*. Some 'props' are required for this session, which the teacher may choose. A telephone is helpful, pieces of paper and buttons are useful for representing money. The drama room should have tables as well as chairs. The meaning of 'sub-text', that is, information which is very important to an understanding of one character, but hidden from other characters on stage, may need some explanation.

Practical Work

1 The teacher should put the props on a table and ask students to choose one to work on in a group. Each student should use the prop in turn but others in the group should decide on a sub-text. For example phoning a friend but being held hostage, dealing cards whilst waiting for news of a relative in hospital, counting money over, knowing that some of it is stolen – by whom? The number of times they can change the sub-text depends on the time available, and the number of students in the group. They may wish to share examples of this work with others to see whether an audience can 'read' the sub-text.

2 The second exercise is based around the use of an alter ego or 'other self' who speaks the sub-text whilst the main character is playing out a scene. One example might be someone trying, politely, to get rid of a guest in order to be alone with a partner. The alter ego would simultaneously be saying all the hurtful things the character is thinking, but dares not say. The same groups could work on these scenes, or students may prefer to change round. After they have tried them out with one central character, they may like to try a situation in which every character has a spoken sub-text. It is not important to share these scenes.

3 Motivation is best applied to every improvisation or piece of text. It is difficult to exercise motivation on its own. The teacher may, however, set up a simple situation such as a family at breakfast and ask the actors to 'freeze' the action at certain points so that they can be questioned about why they did certain things, said certain things or expressed certain attitudes. Another way of extracting motives is to 'hot-seat' a character after a scene has finished. For example, a scene where a factory worker has been dismissed might produce from the character concerned very different reasons for the dismissal than those given in the initial piece of drama.

4 Students should each be given a copy of resource sheet 35 *The Boy with a Cart*. In groups they should go through the chorus and decide what kind of person is speaking at any one time, what peoples' reasons are for being there, what attitudes they have towards the other characters and what sort of occupation they might have, or props they might possess, at that moment. They should then try to place the scene by reading and walking it through. Are there characters in the scene who don't speak? If so, what do they contribute to the scene?

Written Work

Students should be given resource sheet 36 *Launcelot Gobbo*. If necessary it may be read through by the teacher before they begin work on it. They may then write their own version of a 'conscience' *versus* 'devil' speech, either for one of the characters they played in alter-ego exercises, or for a different character.

Students may also like to write a record of the work they undertook, pointing out any successes or difficulties they had with the tasks. They may also choose to make a drawing of *The Boy With a Cart* scene, showing costume, character, position and props.

Follow-up Work

Crowd scenes are a good opportunity to put characterisation into practice. This is especially important when the balance of the action has to fit into the main story, and not detract from it. There are good crowd scenes to be found in many plays, or the class can make up their own, ensuring that characters have a motive for being there and a possible hidden sub-text. Work of this kind should lead into the next lesson.

LESSON 5

Building a Crowd Scene

Working first from illustrations and improvisation and then progressing to work on script is a method that has been used elsewhere in this book. Lesson 5 offers a more ambitious use of this method to conclude Unit 4.

Preparation

> RESOURCE SHEETS 37–38

Students should have at least one copy of the picture on resource sheet 37 between four of them, and an individual copy of resource sheet 38, *A Tale of Two Cities*. The teacher will have to be thoroughly familiar with this scene before working on it with the students.

Practical Work

1 The teacher should organise the students to recreate the scene in the picture on resource sheet 37. It is not necessary to know anything other than that the scene describes a carriage accident and is taken from a novel by Charles Dickens. After they have placed themselves in the position of the people in the scene they may describe themselves in role – for example: 'I am the coachman. It has been a long day and I'm tired.' They may then break up and recreate the scene again, arriving and moving in to the situation in the picture. Once in place they should keep relatively still until everyone is in place. The teacher may have to direct this activity to avoid too much confusion.

2 Students should now have a copy of the script of resource sheet 38, *A Tale of Two Cities* and, after reading it through, should build up the scene both by using the lines that are written down and by illustrating the narrative. This may be done, as in Unit 1, by narrating one's own activity or by illustrating another person's description in silent, or spoken improvisation. Whichever is the more appropriate will become apparent as the scene is worked through; it will probably take the whole of one session to work this out in every detail.

How will the class decide to stage the departure of the Marquis and his carriage?

Written Work

At this stage the teacher may decide to ask students to work on the Unit 4 student assessment form. However, students may also like to write a piece that begins 'I was standing at the street corner by the fountain when. . .'.

Follow-up Work

The scene may be learnt and fully staged. This is a very sophisticated version of the narrative-theatre method used in Unit 1. It might be useful to look back at those exercises and perhaps to rework one of them. The method might be used on another Dickens scene, say from *Oliver Twist*, perhaps the pursuit of Bill Sykes, the theft from Mr Brownlow outside the bookshop or the scenes in Fagin's kitchen. Can students assess what they are now able to add to their staging of such scenes in terms of character, collaborative working, and the ability to shape a scene and select the focus of their action?

Jules Feiffer monologues

1 Bread Crumbs

So I'm going out with this girl for the first time and we're going to the movies and, as usual, I'm throwing out my bread crumbs. And she asks me what is it that I'm doing and I tell her that I'm throwing out bread crumbs so I can find my way home because I have this bad sense of direction. So she laughs like it's a big joke and I say I don't see why my personal troubles should make such a big joke. And she said, "Look—don't worry—I'll take you home!" So I got mad. I said, "Look—we each have our own way of finding ourselves. Who is to say yours is better than mine?" And she said, "You can't make a whole life's philosophy out of bread crumbs." So right out on the street we had a fight. And I got so mad I walked away and I completely forgot to follow my bread crumbs. And an amazing thing happened—I had no trouble getting home. It seems to make my whole past life invalid.

2 I Talk Too Much

I talk too much. I'm quite bright, so it's interesting, but nevertheless, I talk too much. You see, already I'm saying more than I should. Men hate it for a woman to blurt out, "I'm bright." They think she's really saying, "I'm brighter than you are." As a matter of fact, that is what I'm saying. I'm brighter than even the brightest men I know. That's why it's a mistake to talk too much. Men fall behind and feel challenged and grow hostile. So when I'm attracted to a man I make it a point to talk more slowly than I would to one of my woman friends. And because I guide him along gently from insight to insight he ends up being terribly impressed with his own brilliance. And with mine for being able to keep up with him. And he tells me I'm the first woman he's ever met who's as interesting as one of his boy friends. That's love.

Under Milk Wood

Characters
First woman
Second woman
Third woman
Fourth woman

... the women scratch and babble in Mrs Organ Morgan's general shop where everything is sold: custard, buckets, henna, rat-traps, shrimp-nets, sugar, stamps, confetti, paraffin, hatchets, whistles.

FIRST WOMAN	Mrs Ogmore-Pritchard
SECOND WOMAN	la di da
FIRST WOMAN	got a man in Builth Wells
THIRD WOMAN	and he got a little telescope to look at birds
SECOND WOMAN	Willy Nilly said
THIRD WOMAN	Remember her first husband? He didn't need a telescope
FIRST WOMAN	he looked at them undressing through the keyhole
THIRD WOMAN	and he used to shout Tallyho
SECOND WOMAN	but Mr Ogmore was a proper gentleman
FIRST WOMAN	even though he hanged his collie.
THIRD WOMAN	Seen Mrs Butcher Beynon?
SECOND WOMAN	she said Butcher Beynon put dogs in the mincer
FIRST WOMAN	go on, he's pulling her leg
THIRD WOMAN	now don't you dare tell her that, there's a dear
SECOND WOMAN	or she'll think he's trying to pull it off and eat it.
FOURTH WOMAN	There's a nasty lot live here when you come to think.

DYLAN THOMAS

The Fall of Troy

The ruins of a city at dawn. The sun rises slowly over dust, silence and desolation. Amongst the rubble, heaps of rags become visible; they are the women of the city, lying where they may, exhausted, bloodstained and filthy. One cries out in her sleep. One old woman, HECUBA, *begins to drag herself up, using a stick to help her stand.*

HECUBA   Up. Up off the earth. Head up, shoulders straight. Remember who you are. Up. Up on your feet. Come out of your holes, women of Troy. Crawl if you cannot stand. Take a last look at your city. You'll never see it again.

WOMEN   (*variously*) What is it? What has happened? Who is calling? Have they come for us?

HECUBA   Not yet.

WOMEN   Why did you wake us? At least, asleep, we could forget for a while.

HECUBA   Would you rather they dragged you out? Toppled the ruins and buried you alive? Burned the city with you inside?

WOMEN   What does it matter? After last night, what does it matter?

HECUBA   Of course it matters. After last night we are degraded, used... brutally used, scarcely human. Is that how we want them to find us?

WOMEN   How else? They made us like this. They conquered us. They made sure we were beaten, by beating us. They made sure we were humiliated, by humiliating us. They used us like animals so why not stay like animals. You can't expect us to be sweet and gentle after this!

HECUBA   I expect you to be proud.

WOMEN   Proud? Proud of what? Proud of being raped? Perhaps they didn't touch you. Did they leave you? Just because you are ... just because you are a great lady ... or was it because you were too old?

HECUBA   It seems old age is no protection against violence.

WOMEN   You want us to carry on as normal, is that it? Pretend it didn't happen?

HECUBA   No! I want you to show the reality, proudly. I want you to show that we are not beaten.

WOMEN   In spite of them?

HECUBA   Yes.

WOMEN   Bloody but unbowed?

HECUBA   Yes.

WOMEN   Beaten but unconquered.

HECUBA	Yes. Is that too much to ask?
WOMEN	No. We can pull our rags and our dignity together. We can be brave and go out singing. We can follow your lead. You can still be our queen in exile. But what good will it do? How long will they remember? How long can we remember? What will happen to us? Where are we going? Are we going anywhere? Why don't they just finish us off? How do you know they won't topple the ruins and burn us alive with the bodies of our husbands and the corpses of our children?
HECUBA	Whatever happens, I shall meet it as royally as possible. I will not allow them the luxury of seeing me humbled.
WOMEN	Proud words! You will be humbled. They'll make sure of that. If they take us away we'll be made into slaves. You will be a slave! In a foreign country, somebody's slave! Fetching water. Kneeling to fetch water. Kneeling to scrub the floor, kneeling to light the fire. Kneeling to work the fields.

– Women have always done that, knelt at the hearth, knelt at the floor to clean and polish, you've done it, we've done it.

– But then you did it for yourself, for pride in your home, your garden, your children. Pride in yourself.

– That's what Hecuba is saying. We must still have pride in ourselves, in our skill, in our work, in our strength.

– If only we knew what was going to happen. They'll probably decide our fate by the flip of a coin. By the fall of a coin you get to be a nursemaid and I get to be a washerwoman. You work in the fields, I work in the house. Perhaps they'll line us up, feel our muscles, look at our teeth and sell us off in the cattle market. |
HECUBA	And what of me? Where will they take me, this useless drone with the mask of death already upon me? What can I do? Keep my enemy's door or nurse his brats? I, that was Queen of Troy?
WOMEN	They're coming! Soldiers. Men in a hurry. What shall we do? Do we do as we said and meet them proudly? Hecuba?
HECUBA	I can no longer command you. You must do as you think right.

ROSEMARY LINNELL

ANTON CHEKHOV (1860–1904)

Chekhov was a Russian dramatist whose plays have a subtle blend of absurdity and realism that make them immensely popular even today. It was because of the work of the Moscow Arts Theatre that he continued to write full length tragi-comedies about whole groups of characters. There may be leading characters in Chekhov's plays but they require very careful teamwork to make them successful. The director, Stanislavsky (see resource sheet 34) made a great success of *The Seagull* and this was followed by *Uncle Vanya*, *The Cherry Orchard* and *The Three Sisters*.

The Cherry Orchard

CHARLOTTA

[*thoughtfully*]. I don't know how old I am. I haven't got a proper identity card, you see ... and I keep on imagining I'm still quite young. When I was little, father and mother used to tour the fairs and give performances – very good ones they were, too. And I used to jump the *salto-mortale* and do all sorts of other tricks. When Papa and Mamma died, a German lady took me into her house and began to give me lessons. So then I grew up and became a governess. But where I come from and who I am, I don't know. Who my parents were – perhaps they weren't properly married – I don't know. [*She takes a cucumber from her pocket and begins to eat it.*] I don't know anything. [*Pause.*] I'm longing to talk to someone, but there isn't anyone. I haven't anyone. ...

YEPIHODOV

Candidly speaking, and I do want to keep strictly to the point, by the way, but I feel I simply must explain that Fate, so to speak, treats me absolutely without mercy, just like a storm treats a small ship, as it were. I mean to say, supposing I'm wrong, for instance, then why should I wake up this morning and suddenly see a simply colossal spider sitting on my chest? like this. ... [*Makes a gesture with both hands.*] Or supposing I pick up a jug to have a drink of kvass, there's sure to be something frightful inside it, such as a cockroach.

ANTON CHEKHOV

KONSTANTIN STANISLAVSKY (1863–1938)

Stanislavsky founded the Moscow Arts Theatre in Russia, and was one of the world's most influential directors. He wrote several books about acting which are still studied today. His method of studying character before presenting it on the stage gave its name to the Method school of acting in America, of whom Marlon Brando is perhaps the best known exponent.

Stanislavsky taught that an actor must prepare his role in great detail, with a large amount of attention to the psychology, the motivation and the lifestyle of the character, in order to be able to choose significant aspects of action and behaviour to present on the stage. He also reformed the unrealistic style in which productions were staged. Instead of painted trees on a backcloth he would have three-dimensional tree trunks in the foreground even if the ones in the distance were painted. If it was supposed to be snowing or raining outside, then he would make sure that the actors came in with wet coats. It is not so much that Stanislavsky wanted the theatre to be real; it is more that he wanted the audience to forget that they were in a theatre and believe that what they were seeing could really be happening.

Certain phrases have come into use around this style of performance: one is 'the suspension of disbelief', meaning that audiences deliberately leave their real worlds outside and, even though they know that it is only make-believe they want to share the world of the characters on stage: the second phrase is 'the fourth-wall convention' which means that actors and audience behave as if the stage was a room with one wall taken away, so that what is happening inside can be seen by hundreds of people. In every example of this kind of theatre the actors behave as though the audience is not there, whilst at the same time making sure that everyone can see and hear everything. It is a difficult and strange way of behaving but we are used to realism in the theatre, film and television and often suppose that it is, in fact, like real life.

The Boy with a Cart

NEIGHBOURS (*entering*):

One after the other we have gone to the boy,
Offering him advice, condolences, and recommendations
To relations in more well-to-do places.
We have offered him two good meals a day.–
My wife is a bad cook but she gives large helpings.–
We have done what we could; we can't do more.
But he goes his own way. All that we say
He seems to ignore. He keeps himself apart,
Speaking only out of politeness,
Eating out his heart, and of all things on earth
He is making a cart!

One after the other we have gone to him and said,
"Cuthman, what use will a cart be to you?"
He scarcely so much as raised his head, only
Shook it, saying, "I will tell you some other time;
I am in a hurry."

One after the other we have gone also
To his mother, offering advice, condolences,
Recommendations to our distant relations.
His poor mother, she suffers a great deal in her legs.
And we have said to her, "We hope you will excuse
Our asking, we hope you will not think us
Inquisitive, but what is your boy Cuthman
So busy on?" – And she replied each time:
"It is something after his own heart."

We are none the wiser: and after all
It is none of our business, though it's only natural
We should take a certain amount of interest.

One after the other we have gone indoors
Turning it over in our minds as we went
About our chores. What will the old woman do,
Dear heart, with no roof over her head, no man,
No money, and her boy doing nothing
But make a cart?

"I will tell you some other time," he said.
"I am in a hurry." Well, that's his look-out.
It's not for us to worry.

[*They go back to the village.*]

CHRISTOPHER FRY

Launcelot Gobbo

Enter Launcelot.

Certainly my conscience will serve me to run from my master. The fiend is at mine elbow, and tempts me, saying to me, 'Gobbo, Launcelot Gobbo, good Launcelot,' or 'good Gobbo,' or 'good Launcelot Gobbo, use your legs, take the start, run away.' My conscience says, 'No; take heed, honest Launcelot; take heed, honest Gobbo,' or, as aforesaid, 'honest Launcelot Gobbo; do not run; scorn running with thy heels.' Well, the most courageous fiend bids me pack: 'Via!' says the fiend; 'away!' says the fiend; 'for the heavens, rouse up a brave mind,' says the fiend, 'and run.' Well, my conscience, hanging about the neck of my heart, says very wisely to me, 'My honest friend Launcelot, being an honest man's son,' – or rather an honest woman's son; – for, indeed, my father did something smack, something grow to, he had a kind of taste; – well, my conscience says, 'Launcelot, budge not.' 'Budge,' says the fiend. 'Budge not,' says my conscience. 'Conscience,' say I, 'you counsel well;' 'Fiend,' say I, 'you counsel well:' to be ruled by my conscience, I should stay with my master, who, God bless the mark, is a kind of devil; and, to run away, I should be ruled by the fiend, who, saving your reverence, is the devil himself. The fiend gives the more friendly counsel: I will run, fiend; my heels are at your command; I will run.

The Merchant of Venice (abridged) WILLIAM SHAKESPEARE

RESOURCE SHEET 37

Only a Child Run Over

A Tale of Two Cities

With a wild rattle and clatter, and an inhuman abandonment of consideration, the carriage dashed through streets and swept round corners, with women screaming before it, and men clutching each other and clutching children out of its way. At last, swooping at a street corner by a fountain, one of its wheels came to a sickening little jolt, and there was a loud cry from a number of voices, and the horses reared and plunged.

But for the latter inconvenience, the carriage probably would not have stopped; carriages were often known to drive on, and leave their wounded behind, and why not? But the frightened valet had got down in a hurry, and there were twenty hands at the horses' bridles.

'What has gone wrong?' said Monsieur, calmly looking out.

A tall man in a nightcap had caught up a bundle from among the feet of the horses, and had laid it on the basement of the fountain, and was down in the mud and wet, howling over it like a wild animal.

'Pardon, Monsieur the Marquis!' said a ragged and submissive man, 'it is a child.'

'Why does he make that abominable noise? Is it his child?'

'Excuse me, Monsieur the Marquis – it is a pity – yes.'

'Killed!' shrieked the man, in wild desperation, extending both arms at their length above his head, and staring at him. '**Dead!**'

The people closed round, and looked at Monsieur the Marquis. There was nothing revealed by the many eyes that looked at him but watchfulness and eagerness; there was no visible menacing or anger. Neither did the people say anything; after the first cry, they had been silent, and they remained so. The voice of the submissive man who had spoken, was flat and tame in its extreme submission. Monsieur the Marquis ran his eyes over them all, as if they had been mere rats come out of their holes.

He took out his purse.

'It is extraordinary to me,' said he, '**that you people cannot take care of yourselves and your children. One or the other of you is for ever in the way. How do I know what injury you have done my horses? See! Give him that.**'

He threw out a gold coin for the valet to pick up, and all the heads craned forward that all the eyes might look down at it as it fell. The tall man called out again with a most unearthly cry, '**Dead!**'

He was arrested by the quick arrival of another man, for whom the rest made way. On seeing him, the miserable creature fell upon his shoulder, sobbing and crying, and pointing to the fountain, where some women were stooping over the motionless bundle, and moving gently about it. They were as silent, however, as the men.

'I know all, I know all,' said the last comer. '**Be a brave man, my Gaspard! It is better for the poor little plaything to die so, than to live. It has died in a moment without pain. Could it have lived an hour as happily?**'

CHARLES DICKENS

STUDENT ASSESSMENT (UNIT 4)

This unit was mostly about building a character and a good deal of it was personal and needed to be done alone.

1 How did being part of a group help you to build a character for yourself?

2 What did you enjoy most about this work? What do you think you achieved as a result of it?

3 How did the resource material help you to develop characters?

4 Did you find it more satisfying to work on motivation, mood or physical traits, in finding and sustaining a character?

5 How good are you at getting inside a character who is very different from yourself? What difficulties might you find in playing someone who is very like you?

A HODDER AND STOUGHTON MASTER

Unit 5 Performance and a Study of the Actor-Audience Relationship

Available space in school halls and drama rooms is often seen as rather limiting. Quite often it is the imagination that is limited, since most spaces are capable of transformation into a wide variety of performance areas. So long as the drama group are willing to experiment with the actor–audience relationship and to break the traditional mould of Western end-stage performance, then anything is possible.

The five lessons in this unit are expected to run concurrently, with the follow-up (given in Lesson 5, page 97) spread over the weeks up to performance. This is designed to ensure that the groups who are responsible for the end of the story do not suffer from lack of time for preparation.

Some examination schemes do not include any assessment of theatre-arts skills; however a certain amount of attention to sound and light, or costume may be expected. The amount of time spent on design and technical aspects of theatre will therefore depend on the scheme being followed by the school. The degree of teacher intervention may also depend on whether this unit is used to lead directly into an assessed performance or whether it is seen as a way of studying methods which will then be used with another theme for performance before an examiner.

If it is not possible to re-arrange the room totally for every session, it will be necessary for students to make drawings and models of the different types of stage settings. It may be that each student can undertake only one type of staging in a fully finished form, but, as an exercise, it is important that they are all equally aware of the variety of techniques available. In the final performance, it may be possible to use only one or two of the different styles, but if the students have worked through the whole range in theory, then they will, at least, be able to make an informed choice. If there is no time, or materials are not available, then balsa-wood blocks, or childrens' construction bricks may be used as a shortcut towards producing models.

N.B. It is possible to use a 'promenade' style for the final performance that would allow the audience to move around and the actors to use a variety of spaces. This method is outlined in Lesson 4 (page 95) and could be adapted to take in all the other types of staging, provided that there is a large space and that sufficient materials are available.

The resource material in this unit is built around one classic story *The Odyssey* of Homer. Many of these stories were already old when Homer wove them into his epic tale, and there are likely to be many other quest stories, from many other cultures, that would serve as a stimulus for improvisation leading to performance. Much depends on the interests of the group and the availability of source material. The use made of scenes from *The Odyssey* in Unit 5 may be regarded only as a model. Other stories, or other interpretations of this story, may appeal to the group. The teacher is offered this version simply as a series of guidelines towards opening up areas of performance.

LESSON 1

The Lotos-Eaters

The staging for this sequence of the story is that used in the Shakespearian playhouses, where the audience surrounded the stage on three sides. The platform should be high enough so that the audience (whether sitting or standing) has to look up to the action. Entrances are on the fourth side, and scenery and effects may also be placed on that side. The photograph on resource sheet 39 shows students using a high stage, which they surround on three sides.

Preparation

RESOURCE SHEETS 39–40
Rostra or sturdy tables
Optional:
Camera or tape/video recorder

In preparing a story for performance to an audience, the group needs to be made aware of the responsibility they must undertake in selecting images and words that the audience will recognise and respond to with interest and excitement. The interest of the group will have to be kept at a high level and for this reason it is probably best not to tell them the whole story. Naturally there will be someone in the group who knows it all, but nevertheless it is more interesting if each section is dealt with in an entirely different way. The room may be set up as in the photograph on resource sheet 39, or the students may be asked to build a stage out of rostra, or sturdy tables. Each student will need a copy of resource sheets 39 and 40, but the teacher may decide to read the story first, as it is very short.

Practical Work

1 There needs to be quite a time for discussion about the performance element in this unit of work. The teacher should explain that there will be five separate plays, and that each one will be the responsibility of a separate group who will design, direct, light, set to music, costume and act in that one play. In a small group there will have to be some doubling up, but each group of students should take ultimate responsibility for one section of the play. The story will be taken as a theme and it is up to the group to make their own interpretation of it. The teacher should also explain that the thrust-stage method may be abandoned later but is there for experimental purposes. If possible, students should be encouraged to 'say a few words' from the stage and consider the effect of being above the audience, and surrounded by them on three sides, before beginning work on the story.

2 The story should be read over and students given time to discuss the element of addiction that runs through this episode. Three of Odysseus' companions go ashore, so it is possible for three different experiences to be worked on by three groups. The poem *The Lotos-Eaters* by Tennyson on resource sheet 40 offers further ideas about the atmosphere of 'Lotos land' and the nature of the lotos blooms. The students should be asked first to show in slow motion or controlled movement the effect that the lotos drugs had on the people who took them. They may not wish to share this with other groups at this time.

3 Students may now work on a temptation scene. It may be that they see this in terms of a word-picture or as a set of commercials or as an idealised picture of 'Lotos land' in a tableau. Any group finishing ahead of others may like to use the thrust stage to try out this part of their scene. At some stage they may all wish to have a turn on the platform, either to try it out, or to show their work to others.

4 The final scene covers the arrival of Odysseus and his friends, the temptation to join in, and the forcible withdrawal of the three from the effects of the lotos plant. The strength of this scene probably lies in the struggle against giving in, either to the lotos effect or to the pleading of the three to be allowed to continue their habit. This might be a very realistic scene, whether it is performed in modern or legendary terms. The style may even differ between one group and another. The open-stage environment will certainly affect the way they structure their performance, and it will be for the students themselves to sort out the final style. What is important is that the work is recorded in some way, before it is forgotten. It may be scripted, recorded on tape or video, sketched or photographed, or simply headlined by the teacher for future reference but, however memorable it may be at the time, it will not stay very long in the memory unless some way is found of fixing it.

LESSON 2

Circe

The subject matter suggests a 'night-club' type of setting. Even if the students do not see the scene set in this environment, it is a viable way of performing with a mixture of audience and performers in close proximity. The raised 'catwalk' shown in the photograph of students on resource sheet 41 is also used in some Oriental theatrical performances.

Preparation

> RESOURCE SHEETS 41–42
> Chairs
> Optional:
> Raised 'catwalk' area
> Follow-spot on stand
> Camera or tape/video recorder

Each student will require a copy of resource sheets 41 and 42. As in all the other scenes a decision about the most suitable actor–audience relationship will have to be made before the final performance, although audiences can sometimes move about during performances if encouraged by the actors. For the practical session, it may only be necessary to ask the students to set up groups of chairs around the centre of the room so that the performance may take place around them. If a raised acting area can be arranged to run between some of these groups then this will be even more useful. A single follow-spot, on a stand, would lend additional excitement.

Practical Work

1 It would be as well to use the staging in a free-for-all first. This way of staging plays is, in Western terms, unusual; it will become clear that there is no single focus. The photograph (a) on resource sheet 41 shows students working on a raised catwalk which the audience surround, as in photograph (b) of Japanese *Kabuki* theatre. Bearing the design of this stage in mind, students could try out songs, mimes and variety acts in order to practise establishing the focus and drawing audience attention. The advantage of the catwalk is that the action can be very fast, and a change of focus from one actor to another can be achieved simply and effectively. An actor who is out of the picture can just drop away, without having to make an excuse to leave the action.

2 Before starting work on the scene, it might be advisable to do a warm-up exercise. The teacher should remind them of the 'garden-party' exercise and say that they are to represent extremely elegant characters who behave in a rather forced manner but who are given a potion to drink at the party which has the effect of turning them into monsters of depravity. It should be stressed that the 'beast' effect wears off after a few seconds but that the characters will not be sure whether anyone else was affected in the same way, so, although they may resume their forced elegance they will remember that their hands were covered in hair and had talons instead of fingernails, and that they were warped and twisted in their minds and bodies. Having outlined the story, the teacher should organise some signal for the effect of the potion wearing off and announce, 'My Lords and Ladies the party will commence'. After a suitable time the teacher can ask them to drink a toast – 'To His Majesty the King' – and they will drink the potion. This is not to be taken too seriously but it can lead into the work on the Circe story given on resource sheet 41 and illustrated with material on resource sheet 42.

3 After reading the story, and discussing it either in groups or as a whole class, students should be helped to decide whether they want to tackle the whole incident, or whether this makes it too much like the previous scene. It may be that they have very different ideas about what turns sailors into swine! If they want a modern interpretation they will have to decide whether to include Hermes in the story, or to omit that sequence. The teacher will then have to decide whether to divide the class into groups according to different parts of the story, or to let them work in groups of characters; for example, it might be interesting to let the 'sailors' work independently of the 'swine makers' and then to have a confrontation where neither knows what to expect of the other. Alternatively, it may be that they decide to work as a whole class with the teacher as director. Whatever the approach adopted they will need time to work out a way of presenting this story, using the staging to its best advantage.

As in the first lesson in this unit, some record should be made of the scene, especially any particularly effective sequences, for later use.

LESSON 3

The Descent into Hades

Stages in-the-round are very challenging to the actor since there is no 'safe' area in which to get away from the audience, or to switch off for a moment; nevertheless, this method allows a degree of intimacy with the audience which can be very exciting. The descent of Odysseus into Hades is a long sequence and happens at night so that it seems natural to place it in an environment which is capable of depth and darkness. Having the audience raised and looking down on the actors is not a prerequisite of theatre-in-the-round but it should help the actors to get the feel of this scene.

Preparation

> RESOURCE SHEETS 43–44
> Tables or desks
> Optional:
> Rostra

Each student will need a copy of resource sheets 43 and 44 and the room will need to be set up with the action below the audience. This may be achieved by using rostra, or, failing that, by using tables or desks arranged around the acting space with several entrances between them. If it is possible to experiment with lighting, then a system that does not shine directly into the eyes of the audience will have to be devised.

Practical Work

1 Resource sheet 43 shows students working in an improvised theatre-in-the round. It is useful for them to gain an understanding of the challenges offered by this type of staging by arranging the area themselves and experimenting with moves, entrances and sight-lines. What happens when any number of actors remains stationary for any length of time? Is it possible to use furniture in the space? What is the best place for an actor to be, in order to command attention? How large should the space be, in order to obtain the best sight-lines?

2 Having experimented with the environment, students should then be asked to imagine that the space represents a place of shadows. Working in pairs, ask them to fill the space with figures that shadow each other closely. Each one has an alter ego who mirrors a sequence of movements and, perhaps, sound or word patterns endlessly repeated. Homer's Underworld is not full of damned souls, but it is frightening to visit if one is not yet dead. It might be compared to a dream, and it could be helpful to ask students to think of this exercise as part of a dream sequence. It will require quite a command of the space and their own movement to be able to work out this sequence without infringing on other students' work.

3 During a rest from this activity, the teacher could read, or ask the students to read the poems on resource sheet 44 which convey varied impressions of the world of the dead. Against this background of ideas the story of the descent into Hades may be read and discussed. Why would anyone go to this place of dreams? Why does Odysseus go? At what point does Tiresias appear? Is it necessary to have a single figure for the Seer? How important is the ritual sacrifice, and is there a way in which they would like to represent this? If other scenes have been shown in a modern idiom, how do they see a modern version of Hades, or is this scene different because all the shadow figures come from Odysseus's past? How frightening should it be? All these questions and many more will need to be tackled in working on this scene. Students may want to work in small groups, each one handling a different character, or situation, or they may decide to continue the shadowing idea and add to this what they have learned from the story. They may refer back to the work done on ritual earlier in the course (see Unit 2, Lesson 4, page 35). After sufficient preparation time, a way of recording the work should be organised.

LESSON 4

The Sirens, Scylla and Charybdis

Early European theatre used a form of staging which has had a revival in more recent times and is worth examination by the students. There are various titles given to it depending on the environment. If it is out of doors it is usually called street theatre, if it is indoors then it is called promenade theatre and there is a form called *décor simultané*, which is where the audience moves around and the action happens on several distinct acting areas more or less at the same time.

In essence this is a form of theatre in which the actors and the audience occupy the same space. Either of them may take advantage of raised areas in order to see or be seen but the most important factor is that neither is static. Action may begin behind a group of spectators who are standing in a space, they may then turn round or the actors may come through, between them, and play wherever they can. In returning to this ancient style many fluid and exciting, but essentially simple productions have been staged.

Preparation

> RESOURCE SHEETS 45–46
> Tables or platforms
> Optional:
> Camera or tape/video recorder
> Source of music

Three distinct 'stages' are needed for this part of the story, but the main action takes place in the concourse where the audience is supposed to be. The room may be set out with three tables, or high platforms as shown in photograph 1, resource sheets 45–45A. The arrangement of these platforms may be left until the students decide where the Sirens, Scylla and Charybdis should be located, and it is perfectly possible that these scenes can be effectively staged without using platforms at all.

Each student will need a copy of resource sheets 45–45A and 46; as in the other units, some way of recording the work needs to be found.

Practical Work

1 Students should experiment with a variety of ways of making an audience aware of actors who are coming up behind them or appearing from a different side; photograph 2, resource sheet 45A, shows an audience turning round as actors approach. Such simple techniques as sending out a crier to say, 'make room for the actors', is one such device, but they should be encouraged to be inventive. Using music, fanfares, lighting and loud voices provide more sophisticated ways of changing the focus.

2 After a suitable time for experiment they should read the story, on resource sheet 45, and discuss any problems. As before, the interpretation of this scene could veer far from the original and students may consider a wide range of questions before they are divided into four groups. One group will tackle the difficulty inherent in creating a moving ship, if that is what the 'craft' turns out to be; one will create the lure of the Sirens; one Scylla; and one Charybdis. (If it is a small class, the last two may be treated as one.) It is at this point that they may need the three raised areas on which to work.

This section of the legend is the least metaphysical and the most adventurous of all the scenes and it is probably the one which is crying out for a technical approach. The illustration on resource sheet 46, taken from a Greek vase, offers ideas for staging the action: Sound equipment, huge moving figures, masks, ultra-violet light, projected slides or film effects and a wheeled boat are all possible on a limited budget and could be exciting individual or group projects. Much depends on the interest of the group. For the purposes of classroom work, however, their ideas may be worked out in movements that exploit the promenade form, and the ultimate staging can be discussed and recorded in plans, drawings and written descriptions.

LESSON 5

The Homecoming

There is certainly enough material in the Homecoming of Odysseus to create a whole play. Although it may perhaps be difficult to believe that Odysseus's disguise as an old man could really deceive his wife and household, the story is told so that the audience sympathises with him as an individual, human character. The scenes already worked on have, by contrast, tended to concentrate on presenting strong images and ideas rather than individual emotions. The narrative techniques that have been practised several times during this course may well, therefore, be used in this scene to emphasise the difference in style. What is important in telling the story? What should be emphasised and what left out? How should the individual characters be developed? There is a great deal to consider that will serve as a form of revision for the whole course.

Preparation

> RESOURCE SHEETS 47–47A
> Paper and pencils
> Optional:
> Camera or tape/video recorder

End-staging is the most usual form of actor–audience relationship in schools, and there is much to recommend in it, since it is the easiest way of using scenery and furniture. The students may set the room up in this way. They will each need a copy of resource sheet 47–47A.

Practical Work

1 IN PAIRS, members of each pair called A and B for convenience. Students should undertake this work before reading the story on resource sheet 47. A takes the role of a parent and B the adolescent son or daughter. The As go to the teacher and receive quiet instructions that they are to tell the child that they wish to remarry. The Bs are called immediately afterwards and told that they have been offered the unique chance of a year's foreign study, which they would like to take. Neither A nor B should know what the other has been told. They then play out the scene as quietly and as sensitively as they can. There is no need to show these scenes.

2 In the same pairs, or in different pairings, tell them that they are now either estranged husband and wife or estranged parent and child who meet again after twenty years apart. All they have to decide before playing the scene is which relationship they choose. They should be told that at first they are very ill at ease with each other. They may be reminded of the scene about the children, separated by the boundaries between nations, and if they wish they may repeat the idea of concentrating on hands as a means of establishing contact. Again there is no need to show these scenes.

3 After some talk about the way these scenes were handled, and some exchange of information about whether they were able to relate to each other after so long an absence, the class should read through and discuss the homecoming story on resource sheet 47. Every one of the major characters is reluctant to go into abrupt action; they all feel the need to move gently round the situation first. Students may be able to work out their own motivation for this delicacy without discussion, or they may need help in talking it out before improvising scenes.

4 It may not be helpful at this stage to put the whole story of the homecoming together. It could be that these conversations provide enough raw material for the group who will eventually handle this sequence in performance. On the other hand there may be time to structure the whole scene. Students would then have to decide whether to include the routing of the suitors in their play, or whether to end the whole story on a rather more intimate and quiet note.

Follow-up Material and Written Work

Final rehearsed improvisation based on a text

Although the story of Odysseus is, on the face of it, a very masculine story, there is enough opportunity for wide interpretation. It would be very tedious if everyone were to take this material simply on its face value. It is submitted here merely as an example. On this basis, the obvious way to proceed would be to allow each group to work on one of the five scenes and to determine their own method of presentation. Exactly the same method could be applied to any material of similar epic proportions. The teacher may facilitate the students' own work by organising appropriate warm-up exercises, providing music, or the means of creating it, enabling groups to work apart from the others if space allows, providing materials for creating masks, figures or costumes if such are required, and generally motivating the weak-hearted and coping with the frustrations that absenteeism and poor co-operation inevitably create. In some cases, a firm hand may have to be taken over cutting scenes that are not being handled constructively. Good students may be unduly penalised by being paired with the unco-operative ones and some shuffling of numbers may be needed at an early stage. They will probably work best in their own peer groups at this late stage in the course, and a wise teacher will allow them to do so. It also means that the high flyers can be allowed to get on in their own way whilst time can be spent working with those who need encouragement, if not direct help. Some careful bringing together of the whole piece by means of narration, lighting, and perhaps a linking character (although that poses rehearsal problems), should be the teacher's responsibility.

As little time as possible should be spent on rehearsing. The importance of recording the scenes during the preliminary work will help to cut down on trying to reconstruct a long-forgotten scene. If each group only has to work on one short sequence and build that up to whatever seems reasonable, they should not get bored.

Written work should be in the form of designs, scripts (if needed), narration, poems, songs, and rituals. Anything which is produced may be used in the final performance or simply added to the student's own folder. After the performance the students should be encouraged to make an assessment of the whole experience using, if convenient, the student's end-of-unit assessment form for Unit 5. In addition, some students may enjoy keeping a running record of the production in words, photographs and drawings, rather in the style of 'the film about the making of the film'. This may seem an unlikely occupation in the flurry of final preparations for performance, but it can provide a few moments of calm and a chance to reflect on the process as well as on the product, and is often time well spent.

RESOURCE SHEET 39

ODYSSEUS

Odysseus was a perpetual trickster and gipsy who invented the wooden horse that ended the Trojan War. He wandered many years after the battle, having offended certain gods: Poseidon who caused rough seas, and Aeolius who brought contrary winds. Disaster dogged his journey and cost him his entire crew and almost his life, before he could rejoin his family.

The Lotos Isles

After days and nights of the fiercest, god-angered storms, Odysseus and his crew came upon the coastline of the Lotos Isles. Glad to find ease and rest in the gentle sun, they landed to take on water. The whole ship's crew came on shore for the midday meal, and the captain sent out a party to discover what sort of people lived there. Soon enough they fell in with some of the lotos-eaters, who were only too eager to press the sweet lotos plant upon them, encouraging them to take their fill. Those who take this honey-sweet plant, the lotos, find it has a fatal effect. They become addicted to it, they forget their old life, their friends, everything. All they want is to have more, and yet more of the lotos.

When Odysseus found them in this state he was angry and drove them, wailing, crying and shaking, back to the ship. They even had to be tied down to prevent them running back, so far had the lotos taken possession of their senses.

Students working with a thrust-stage

The Lotos-Eaters

'Courage!' he said, and pointed toward the land,
'This mounting wave will roll us shoreward soon.'
In the afternoon they came unto a land
In which it seemed always afternoon.

There is sweet music here that softer falls
Than petals from blown roses on the grass,
Or night-dews on still waters between walls
Of shadowy granite, in a gleaming pass;
Music that gentlier on the spirit lies,
Than tir'd eyelids upon tir'd eyes;
Music that brings sweet sleep down from the blissful skies.
Here are cool mosses deep,
And thro' the moss the ivies creep,
And in the stream the long-leaved flowers weep,
And from the craggy ledge the poppy hangs in sleep.

The Lotos blooms below the barren peak:
The Lotos blows by every winding creek:
All day the wind breathes low with mellower tone:
Thro' every hollow cave and alley lone
Round and round the spicy downs the yellow Lotos-dust is blown.

(abridged) ALFRED LORD TENNYSON

RESOURCE SHEET 41

Circe

So fearful were Odysseus and his companions about what they might encounter at their next landfall that they grouped themselves into two parties and drew lots as to who was to guard the ship and who should go in search of food.

The search party saw smoke rising from a house and made towards it. They were amazed to find the place surrounded by fierce beasts who lay as if drugged or under the spell of the sweet music that came from inside the building. The sailors found themselves drawn towards the singing and, all except their leader, they disappeared through the open door, into the house of Circe, the enchantress.

Once inside, they were completely taken in by Circe and her attendants. They lounged on couches, ate, drank and were so seduced that, before long, Circe could do as she wished with them. She drove them, grunting and swinish into a foul pigsty where there was filthy mud to lie on and where they fed on acorns and berries.

When Odysseus heard that his crew was missing he went alone to Circe's house. On the way he met the messenger of the gods, Hermes, who gave him the root of the plant Moly, as a charm against Circe's wiles. Try as she might, her spells had no effect on Odysseus and he was able to force her to release the others from the sty. Far from fleeing the place, he ordered the ship to be pulled up on shore so that the entire crew might be entertained in safety.

a Students working with a catwalk stage

b Japanese *Kabuki* theatre

A HODDER AND STOUGHTON MASTER

Moly

Nightmare of beasthood, snorting, how to wake.
I woke. What beasthood skin she made me take?

Leathery toad that ruts for days on end,
Or cringing dribbling dog, man's servile friend,

Or cat that prettily pounces on its meat,
Tortures it hours, then does not care to eat:

Parrot, moth, shark, wolf, crocodile, ass, flea.
What germs, what jostling mobs there were in me.

   These seem like bristles, and the hide is tough.
No claw or web here: each foot ends in hoof.

Into what bulk has method disappeared?
Like ham, streaked. I am gross — grey, gross, flap-eared.

The pale-lashed eyes my only human feature.
My teeth tear, tear. I am the snouted creature

That bites through anything, root, wire, or can.
If I was not afraid I'd eat a man.

Oh a man's flesh already is in mine.
Hand and foot poised for risk. Buried in swine.

   I root and root, you think that it is greed,
It is, but I seek out a plant I need.

Direct me gods, whose changes are all holy,
To where it flickers deep in grass, the moly:

Cool flesh of magic in each leaf and shoot,
From milky flower to the black forked root.

From this fat dungeon I could rise to skin
And human title, putting pig within.

I push my big grey wet snout through the green,
Dreaming the flower I have never seen.

THOM GUNN

Circe offering Odysseus a bowl of drugged wine. A painting on a vase dating from the first quarter of the 5th century B.C.

RESOURCE SHEET 43

Hades

After the feasting Circe advised Odysseus that the only way to rid himself of the fury of the gods was to seek advice from the spirit of the prophet Tiresias. His was one of those spirits who dwelt on the shores of the world, in the Land of the Dead. To go there whilst still alive was to undertake the most terrible journey that anyone could suffer, but Odysseus had no option but to go.

The whole crew set sail and eventually landed upon the dark shore in the dead of night. Odysseus drew away from the others and made a ritual sacrifice, pouring wine, white barley meal and the black blood of slain animals upon the ground. He drew his sword and waited, sick with fear, for the spirit of Tiresias to appear. All around he could hear the multitude of souls that shadowed the air, moaning and crying. More terrifying still he could discern the spirit of his mother, whom he had thought to be alive and well. He saw her clearly, but she could not recognise him and slipped, insubstantial, through his grasp when he tried to embrace her.

Finally Tiresias appeared with a golden sceptre in his hand. He had little hope for Odysseus. Storms and winds, whirlpool and wreck, his wife besieged by riotous suitors, his son, now nearly grown, searching desperately for news of the father he could scarcely remember while trying to protect his mother. . .so it went on until the crowding shadows of the dead filled the night with their cries of murder and violent death, of sorrow and sad loneliness. Finally Odysseus resumed his journey, back to the known dangers of the living world.

Students working with a sunken theatre-in-the-round

And Death Shall Have No Dominion

And death shall have no dominion.
Dead men naked they shall be one
With the man in the wind and the west moon;
When their bones are picked clean and the clean bones gone,
They shall have stars at elbow and foot;
Though they go mad they shall be sane,
Though they sink through the sea they shall rise again;
Though lovers be lost love shall not;
And death shall have no dominion.

And death shall have no dominion.
Under the windings of the sea
They lying long shall not die windily;
Twisting on racks when sinews give way,
Strapped to a wheel, yet they shall not break;
Faith in their hands shall snap in two,
And the unicorn evils run them through;
Split all ends up they shan't crack;
And death shall have no dominion.

And death shall have no dominion.
No more may gulls cry at their ears
Or waves break loud on the seashores;
Where blew a flower may a flower no more
Lift its head to the blows of the rain;
Though they be mad and dead as nails,
Heads of the characters hammer through daisies;
Break in the sun till the sun breaks down,
And death shall have no dominion.

DYLAN THOMAS

From *Paradise Lost*

The dismal situation waste and wild.
A dungeon horrible, on all sides round,
As one great furnace flamed; yet from those flames
No light; but rather darkness visible
Served only to discover sights of woe,
Regions of sorrow, doleful shades, where peace
And rest can never dwell, hope never comes
That comes to all, but torture without end
Still urges, and a fiery deluge, fed
With ever-burning sulphur unconsumed.

(abridged) JOHN MILTON

RESOURCE SHEET 45

Sirens, Scylla and Charybdis

Events crowded so fast on Odysseus and his crew that scarcely could they draw breath before the latest danger was upon them. The song of the sirens could not be resisted, so the sailors had to plug their ears with softened beeswax and Odysseus had to have himself tied to the mast until they were past the place where the skeletons of other unfortunate sailors lay piled upon the shore.

Then it was but a moment before they came to the wandering rocks where even the doves who fly past are dashed to pieces against the cliffs, where on the one hand is the whirlpool of Charybdis, forever roaring and sucking down the salt seas, and on the other Scylla, the six-headed monster, against whom no defence is possible. It was only by forcing their ship at full speed between the two that they avoided total disaster. Even so, six of the crew were killed.

Students working with three separate stages

RESOURCE SHEET 45A

Actors approaching their audience from behind

An audience surrounding a street theatre performance

RESOURCE SHEET 46

Odysseus has himself tied to the mast to resist the Sirens.
A painting on a vase dating from the first quarter of the 5th century B.C.

The Homecoming

At last Odysseus reached the shores of Ithaca and entered his court disguised as an old man.

He found that things were indeed as Tiresias had foretold. Telemachus, his son had returned from a fruitless search for his father, the nobles were pursuing Penelope, his wife, and squandering his wealth. Penelope had delayed giving an answer while she still had hope that Odysseus would return. At first she had pretended that she must finish her weaving, so she wove all day and undid the work at night but this ruse was discovered and now she was beginning to lose faith. Finally, she said that she would marry the man who could string the bow that Odysseus had left behind and shoot an arrow with it.

Odysseus revealed his identity to Telemachus and they secretly removed all the nobles' weapons from the hall. He was also recognised by an old maidservant but he made her swear to keep the secret and to keep Penelope away during the contest.

The suitors tried to bend the bow, but failed. Odysseus was mocked as an old fool when he came forward but he easily strung the bow and shot the arrow. A fight ensued, but with all their weapons gone the suitors were soon vanquished.

At first husband and wife were ill at ease with each other. It took some time and many assurances, even after Odysseus had removed his disguise, before they were able to resume their relationship.

Penelope with her son Telemachus and, in the background, her loom with the unfinished web. A painting on a vase dated about 450 B.C.

RESOURCE SHEET 47A

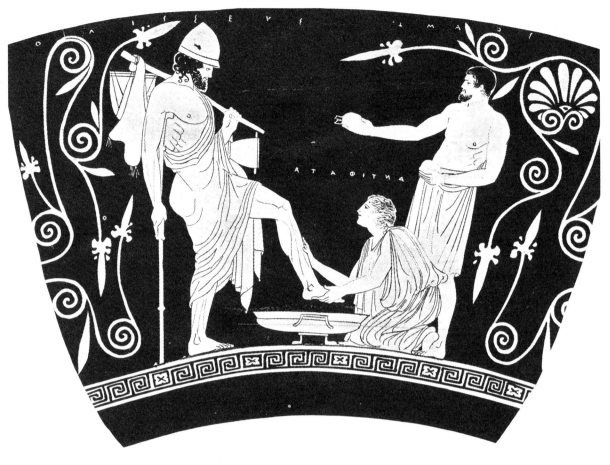

Odysseus, dressed as a beggar, having his feet washed by Eurycleia. A painting from a vase dated about 440 B.C.

Odysseus takes his revenge on Penelope's suitors. A painting from the inside of a cup; about 450–440 B.C.

A HODDER AND STOUGHTON MASTER

STUDENT ASSESSMENT UNIT 5)

Performance on a variety of stages was the focus for this work.

1 How do you assess the importance of performing to an audience?

2 Which kind of staging did you find the most exciting during the classwork? Do you think it was the best from the audience's point of view?

3 Do you think you were best at performing other people's ideas, or at turning your own ideas into a piece of theatre? Are you able to switch easily from being an actor to being a director?

4 How useful is it to look at other forms of art in deciding how to convey an idea to an audience? Which of the resources were particularly helpful to you?

5 Was there a particular interest in any of the work that you would like to have taken further? What do you think you achieved as a result of working on this unit?

EVALUATION AND ASSESSMENT SHEET FOR TEACHERS

The following questions may be used as a guide to teachers in evaluating a student's achievement in a given unit of work. Many examination syllabuses set their own assessment criteria, and these may be taken in conjunction with the following suggestions, whenever a student's work is being assessed as part of an examination course.

1 Did the student appreciate the objectives that were set in this unit?

2 Was the student's attitude to the work positive?

3 Was the student willing to accept responsibility for individual work, and written work?

4 Did the student accept a positive part in the practical work?

5 Was the student open to suggestions from the peer group and from the teacher?

6 Was the student sensitive and attentive to the needs and contributions of others in the group?

7 Was the student able to focus upon the task in hand and direct the work towards appropriate objectives?

8 Did the student make progress in developing or acquiring further skills?

9 Was the student able to evaluate personal or group achievement in the work undertaken as part of this unit?

10 Was the student punctual and regular in attendance?